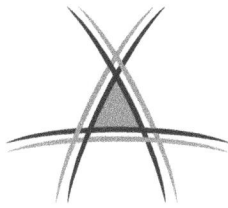

ASCENT
CENTER FOR TECHNICAL KNOWLEDGE

Autodesk® Revit® 2023
Site Planning and Design

Learning Guide
Metric Units - 1st Edition

ASCENT - Center for Technical Knowledge®
Autodesk® Revit® 2023
Site Planning and Design
Metric Units - 1st Edition

Prepared and produced by:

ASCENT Center for Technical Knowledge
630 Peter Jefferson Parkway, Suite 175
Charlottesville, VA 22911

866-527-2368
www.ASCENTed.com

Lead Contributor: Cherisse Biddulph

Contents

Preface

The objective of the *Autodesk® Revit® 2023: Site Planning and Design* guide is to enable users who have worked with the Autodesk Revit software to understand concepts and tools related to site planning and design. This guide covers the Revit coordinate system, which is used to coordinate multiple files in a single project, as well as the elements and tools that are used to create topographic surfaces for site work.

Topics Covered

- Site Planning
  - Understanding the Revit coordinate system, positioning, true north, and project north.
  - Linking files.
  - Relocating the project elevation.
  - Working with shared coordinates by acquiring and publishing coordinates.
  - Exporting Revit models to .DWG.
- Site Design
  - Creating topographic surfaces.
  - Adding property lines and building pads.
  - Modifying toposurfaces with subregions, splitting surfaces, and grading the regions.
  - Annotating site plans and adding site components.

Prerequisites

- Access to the 2023.0 version of the software, to ensure compatibility with this guide. Future software updates that are released by Autodesk may include changes that are not reflected in this guide. The practices and files included with this guide might not be compatible with prior versions (e.g., 2022).

- Knowledge of the basic techniques of the fundamentals of the Autodesk Revit software covered in the *Autodesk Revit 2023: Fundamentals for Architecture* guide.

Note on Learning Guide Content

ASCENT's learning guides are intended to teach the technical aspects of using the software and do not focus on professional design principles and standards. The exercises aim to demonstrate the capabilities and flexibility of the software, rather than following specific design codes or standards, which can vary between regions.

Note on Software Setup

This guide assumes a standard installation of the software using the default preferences during installation. This includes the Revit templates and Revit Content (Families) that can be found on the Autodesk website at https://knowledge.autodesk.com/ by searching **How to download Revit Content**. Lectures and practices use the standard software templates and default options.

Lead Contributor: Cherisse Biddulph

Cherisse is an Autodesk Certified Professional for Revit as well as an Autodesk Certified Instructor. She brings over 19 years of industry, teaching, and technical support experience to her role as a Learning Content Developer with ASCENT. With a passion for design and architecture, she received her Associates of Applied Science in Drafting and Design and has worked in the industry assisting firms with their CAD management and software implementation needs as they modernize to a Building Information Modeling (BIM) design environment. Although her main passion is the Revit design product, she is also proficient in AutoCAD, Autodesk BIM 360, and Autodesk Navisworks. Today, Cherisse continues to expand her knowledge in the ever-evolving AEC industry and the software used to support it.

Cherisse Biddulph has been the Lead Contributor for *Autodesk Revit: Site Planning and Design* since 2020.

In This Guide

The following highlights the key features of this guide.

Feature	Description
Practice Files	The Practice Files page includes a link to the practice files and instructions on how to download and install them. The practice files are required to complete the practices in this guide.
Chapters	A chapter consists of the following: Learning Objectives, Instructional Content, Practices, Chapter Review Questions, and Command Summary.
	• **Learning Objectives** define the skills you can acquire by learning the content provided in the chapter.
	• **Instructional Content**, which begins right after Learning Objectives, refers to the descriptive and procedural information related to various topics. Each main topic introduces a product feature, discusses various aspects of that feature, and provides step-by-step procedures on how to use that feature. Where relevant, examples, figures, helpful hints, and notes are provided.
	• **Practice** for a topic follows the instructional content. Practices enable you to use the software to perform a hands-on review of a topic. It is required that you download the practice files (using the link found on the Practice Files page) prior to starting the first practice.
	• **Chapter Review Questions**, located close to the end of a chapter, enable you to test your knowledge of the key concepts discussed in the chapter.
	• **Command Summary** concludes a chapter. It contains a list of the software commands that are used throughout the chapter and provides information on where the command can be found in the software.

Practice Files

To download the practice files for this guide, use the following steps:

1. Type the URL *exactly as shown below* into the address bar of your Internet browser, to access the Course File Download page.

    Note: If you are using the ebook, you do not have to type the URL. Instead, you can access the page simply by clicking the URL below.

    https://www.ascented.com/getfile/id/limiaPF

2. On the Course File Download page, click the **DOWNLOAD NOW** button, as shown below, to download the .ZIP file that contains the practice files.

3. Once the download is complete, unzip the file and extract its contents.

    The recommended practice files folder location is:
    C:\Revit Site Planning and Design Practice Files

    Note: It is recommended that you do not change the location of the practice files folder. Doing so may cause errors when completing the practices.

Stay Informed!

To receive information about upcoming events, promotional offers, and complimentary webcasts, visit:

www.ASCENTed.com/updates

Site Planning

Site planning and design collaboration is an involved and thoughtful process. A good graphical representation of the site's topography in the correct coordinate location greatly helps in the designing and placement of a building on a site.

Autodesk® Revit® has a coordinate system with the capabilities of establishing a mutual location for linked files within the host model called shared coordinates. This is achieved by acquiring coordinates from a linked toposurface or files from a civil engineer or a surveyor. This shared coordinate location can then be published from the host model to the linked files. Revit shared coordinates work to align multiple projects from different disciplines and software applications into one project location and maintain the relationship between them all.

Learning Objectives in This Chapter

- Learn about internal origin, project base point, and survey point.
- Understand coordinates, positioning, true north, and project north.
- Share, publish, and acquire coordinates.
- Relocate the project's elevation.

1.1 Preparing a Project for Site Design

This workflow may vary depending on your company standards.

A typical project workflow will be established by your company's BIM/project manager, but may include the following:

- Model coordination (e.g., internal origin to internal origin, project base point, or shared coordinates) is typically determined at the kick-off meeting using a BIM execution plan.

- Establish the project base point and drawing units in your Revit model. Acquire coordinates from a linked file containing survey information and publish coordinates if collaborating using shared coordinates.

- Understand Revit import/linking options and positioning to facilitate creating the project site. Link necessary files into the Revit model using import/linking options. Acquire coordinates, create topography, and/or facilitate creating the project site.

- If needed, provide the civil engineer or surveyor with an exported .DWG file from your Revit host model of the preliminary site layout so they can prepare the site. The civil engineer may include the survey and project base points (with the architect's approval). They should also include a toposurface or CAD file to help build a site plan in Revit.

- Create a site or topography (e.g., add a building pad, parking lots, and site and parking components like trees, shrubs, and cars).

Terminology

It is important to understand the following terms before working with shared coordinates. Reference these definitions as you go through this guide to help clarify what each term is referring to.

- **Survey Coordinate System:** Displays in the Revit view as the survey point and is intended to display the location on the earth's surface.

- **Project Coordinate System:** Displays in the Revit view as the project base point and is intended to display the location of the building model.

- **Host Model:** The primary model into which other files and models are linked (i.e., the site model or composite building model).

- **Shared Coordinates:** When you have multiple linked buildings, you can use shared coordinates to remember the respective positions of your buildings. Only the host Revit model (i.e., the site model or composite building model) should be used for obtaining shared coordinates.

  - If the required coordinates for the project are in a linked model/file, you will acquire the coordinates or pull the coordinates from the linked file.
  - If the required coordinates for the project are in the host model, you will publish coordinates or push your model's coordinates to the linked models/files.

- **Acquiring Coordinates:** Acquiring or pulling survey coordinates from a linked file will establish the shared coordinate system for the host model.

- **Publishing Coordinates:** Publishing or pushing survey coordinates from the host file to any linked files or models will establish the shared coordinate system for the linked files.

- **Positioning:** When linking in other models or files, use the positioning options in the Import or Link dialog box to specify where you would like the information placed relative to your host model. There are two types: Automatic (Auto) and Manual.

  - **Auto** is best used when you know the coordinates of the host model and the imported/linked model or file. Auto positioning uses a set of rules to place the incoming geometry in an exact location based on coordinates.
  - **Manual** is best used when you want to use a point that is defined in the linked/imported file. Using manual positioning gives you more control over the placement of incoming geometry.

- **Internal Origin:** The internal origin is the starting point for the internal coordinates system, which provides the basis for positioning all elements in the model. This is also known as the startup location and it never moves from its original location. By default, the internal origin is turned off in all views.

- **Project Base Point:** Defines the origin of the project coordinate system. The project base point will change based on the origin point of the survey point. The project base point can be used for coordination on a project by positioning it at a useful place, such as the intersection of grid lines or the corner of a building.

- **Survey Point:** Defines the real world or global coordinate system. It is typically a specific point in the physical environment, such as the intersection of property lines or a survey marker. It is used to establish shared coordinates between multiple linked files.

- **Named Positions:** When working with multiple buildings that are either copied within the project or linked into the project, you can set up named positions to maintain their location in the project.

- **True North:** This is your project's location in regards to the real world coordinates. You can create a view to graphically display your model in true north.

- **Project North:** This is your project's location in regards to the paper or screen you are modeling on, typically at 90 degrees. You will usually draw with your view set to project north.

Hint: Revit Tooltips

To learn more about each tool's function, from the *Manage* tab> Project Location panel, hover your cursor over the tool to display a tooltip describing its use and a GIF showing that use in action, as shown in Figure 1–1.

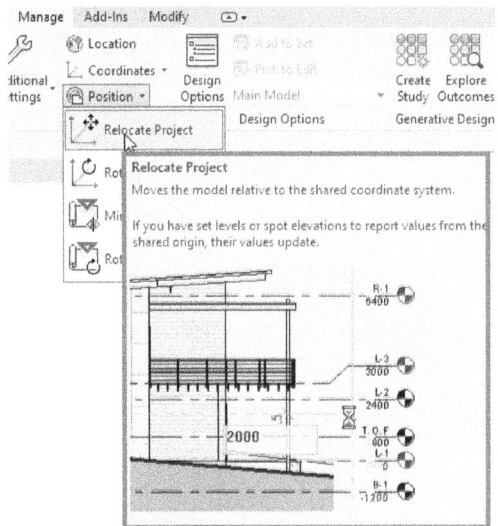

Figure 1–1

1.2 Coordinate System in Revit

All Revit projects have an internal coordinate system called internal origin or startup location. All elements in the model are positioned according to the internal origin. The project and survey coordinate systems are based off of the internal origin and are specified in a view by the ⊗ (Project Base Point) and

⚠ (Survey Point) icons, as shown in Figure 1–2. These points, by default, are located at Revit's internal origin but can be moved according to shared coordinates and building locations.

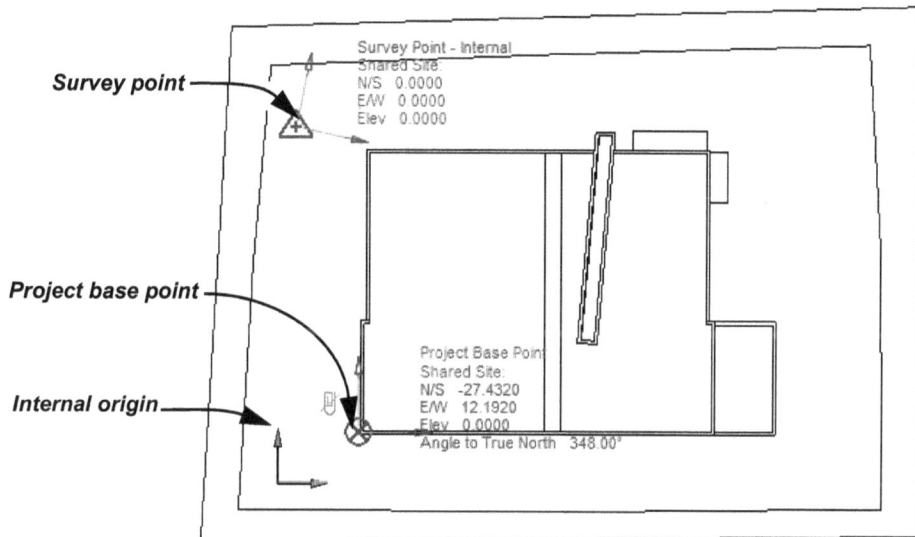

Survey point

Survey Point - Internal
Shared Site:
N/S 0.0000
E/W 0.0000
Elev 0.0000

Project base point

Project Base Point
Shared Site:
N/S -27.4320
E/W 12.1920
Elev 0.0000
Angle to True North 348.00°

Internal origin

Figure 1–2

- The internal origin location will never move. Any modeled geometry needs to be within a **16km** radius from the internal origin to avoid unwelcome behavior (e.g., graphical issues or model stability).

- The project base point is for your model's internal use and shows the coordinates based on its distance from the survey point, reflecting the project coordinate system. The project base point impacts levels, label contours, and absolute elevations, as well as what is reported using the **Spot Elevation** and **Spot Coordinate** commands.

- The survey point is usually placed relative to the site of a project and defines the project's true north Y-axis. If given the coordinates from a surveyor or engineer, you can manually specify the survey point coordinates directly in your model. If a file is provided, you can acquire coordinates from linking it into your model.

When starting from a default architectural template and opening the site view, the ⊗ (Project Base Point) and ⟁ (Survey Point) icons both show and by default are located at Revit's internal origin location, causing the icons to overlap (as shown in Figure 1–3). You can display the internal origin by turning it on through the Visibility/Graphic Overrides under the Site category.

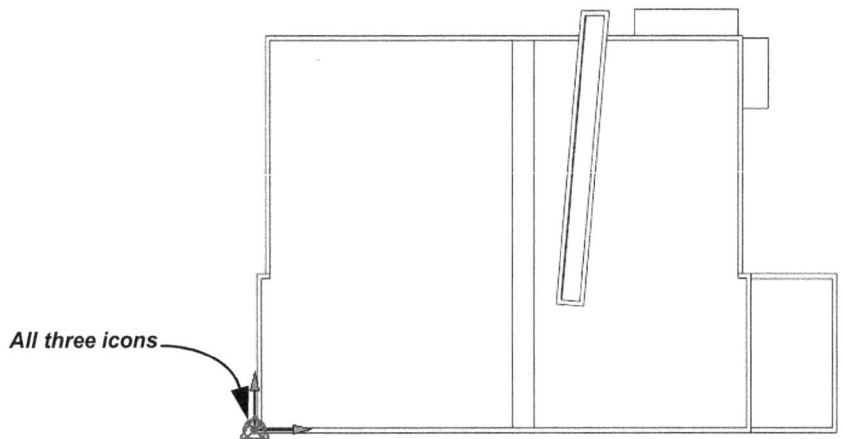

All three icons

Figure 1–3

Identifying Coordinates

To help you understand where things are located within the project and its linked file(s), use the **Report Shared Coordinates** tool. To identify a coordinate point, in the *Manage* tab>Project Location panel, expand ⌐ (Coordinates) and click ⌐ (Report Shared Coordinates). ⌐ displays on the cursor. Move it over a point on the project and click it. The shared coordinates display in the Options Bar, as shown in Figure 1–4.

| N/S: 24338.6 | E/W: -3.4 | Elevation: 1200.0 |

Figure 1–4

- To move the project to new coordinates, change the project base point or click ⌐ (Specify coordinates at point).

Modify Coordinates Individually

You can specify the project base point and survey point by entering in the coordinates or manually moving them. This can be done if you have been given the site coordination from the civil engineer or surveyor, or if the project is being done internally in one office. Once moved, you can reset back to the internal origin, as well as reset the shared coordinates if coordinates need to be re-established.

*   To modify the project base point, click on the icon and modify *N/S*, *E/W*, *Elev*, and *Angle to True North*, as shown in Figure 1–5. Alternatively, you can set up the values in Properties, as shown in Figure 1–6.

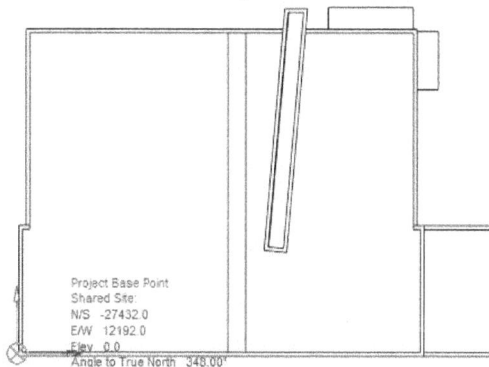

Figure 1–5

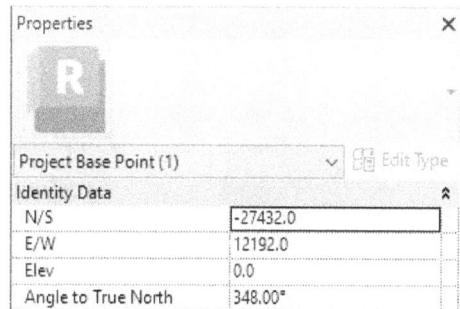

Figure 1–6

*   To manually modify the survey point, you will have to unclip it and then edit the *N/S*, *E/W*, and *Elev*, as shown in Figure 1–7. Alternatively, you can modify the values in Properties, as shown in Figure 1–8.

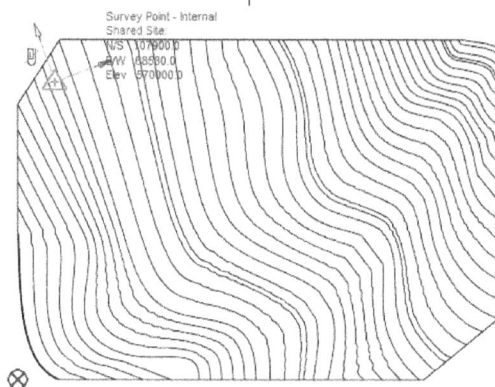

Figure 1–7

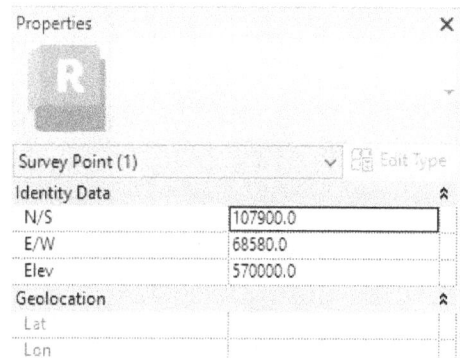

Figure 1–8

- ⬚ (Change clip state of point) displays next to the survey point and indicates whether it is clipped or unclipped. If ⬚ is displayed beside the survey point, the survey point is clipped. If the survey point is moved while it is clipped, the origin of the project will change, which will affect the project base point. The internal coordinate system will always remain the same. The project base point will update according to the origin of the survey point. Should the survey point become unclipped and be moved, it will base its coordinates upon the internal origin and the project base point does not change.

- If ⬚ is displayed beside the survey point, the survey point is unclipped. If the survey point is unclipped and moved, the project coordinates change but the model elements do not move.

How To: Reset the Project Base Point

If you want to reset the project base point to the internal origin, select ⊗ (Project Base Point), right-click, and select **Move to Internal Origin**, as shown in Figure 1–9.

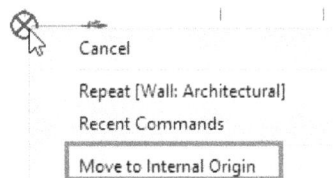

Figure 1–9

- The project base point relocates to the internal origin location.

How To: Reset the Survey Point

If you want to reset the survey point after moving it or acquiring shared coordinates, from the *Manage* tab>Project Location panel, select ⬚ (Reset Shared Coordinates).

- The survey point relocates to the internal origin location.

- Resetting the survey point allows you to re-acquire coordinates from a linked file.

1.3 Linking Files

The position of linked files needs to be established to keep the relationship between all files cohesive. In this section, you will learn about the process of linking models, what positionings are available, and how they respond to your host Revit model. When you link a Revit model, any views displaying the host's survey point and project base point will display the icons in blue, and the linked model's project base point and survey point icons will be grayed out, as shown in Figure 1–10. CAD files that have been linked into the project will not show any base points unless they have been drawn in or annotated.

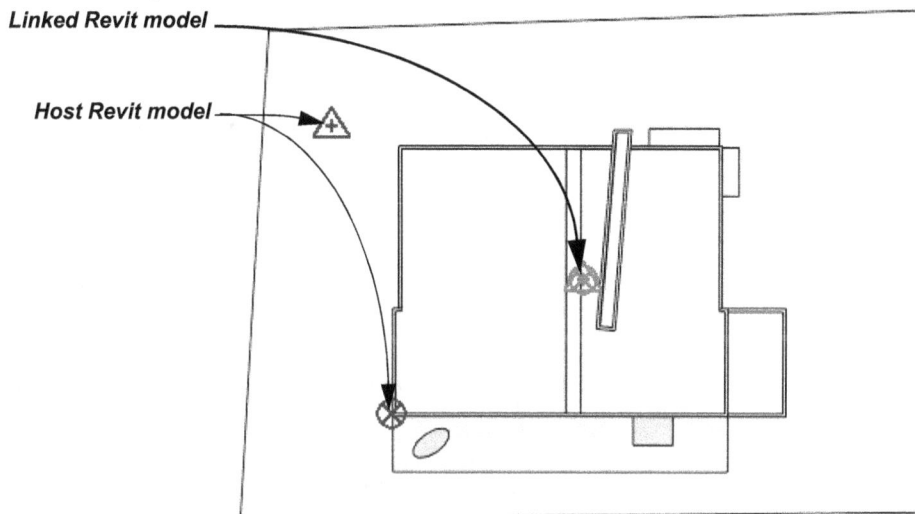

Linked Revit model

Host Revit model

Figure 1–10

- Any linked model automatically updates if the original file is changed.

- Models created in Revit need to be created from the same release cycle (i.e., created either with Revit 2023 (initial installation build) or with an update installed, such as Revit 2023.1).

- CAD file formats that can be imported or linked include AutoCAD® (DWG and DXF), MicroStation (DGN), 3D ACIS modeling kernel (SAT), Trimble SketchUp (SKP), and McNeel Rhino (3DM) (import only).

Link Model/File Positioning

Linking vs. Importing

- **Linking:** A connection is maintained with the original file and the link updates if the original file is updated. If you plan to publish or acquire coordinates from a linked model or file, you will want to use the linking method.

- **Importing:** No connection is maintained with the original linked CAD file. It becomes a separate element in the Revit model. You cannot publish or acquire coordinates from imported files. However, imported files are used to create toposurfaces within Revit. See *2.1 Creating Topographical Surfaces* for more on creating toposurfaces.

There are several link positioning options to choose from for both CAD and Revit files, as shown in Figure 1–11. Check with your BIM manager on the method they have decide to use for linking in models and files to maintain the relationship of each model.

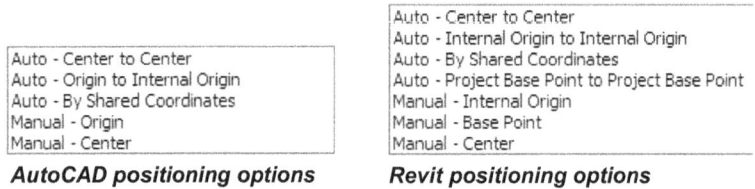

```
Auto - Center to Center
Auto - Origin to Internal Origin
Auto - By Shared Coordinates
Manual - Origin
Manual - Center
```

```
Auto - Center to Center
Auto - Internal Origin to Internal Origin
Auto - By Shared Coordinates
Auto - Project Base Point to Project Base Point
Manual - Internal Origin
Manual - Base Point
Manual - Center
```

AutoCAD positioning options   *Revit positioning options*

Figure 1–11

Link Positioning Options

Auto - Center to Center	This option provides a way to link CAD files when the origin is miles away from Revit's internal origin.
Auto - Internal Origin to Internal Origin	Used to align models with their own internal origin. This is useful to use when aligning the architectural model with the structural model, for example.
Auto - By Shared Coordinates	This option is usually only used when shared coordinates have already been activated.
Auto - Project Base Point to Project Base Point	This option aligns two Revit models' project base points. This is the preferred approach as it allows the building models (architectural, MEP, and structural) to align even if they are in different locations from the internal origin, so long as they have their project base points set up correctly. Note that this option can get dangerous due to project base points being moved.
Manual options	All manual options are not as accurate as the auto options, so they are not used as much when working with shared coordinates.

How To: Add a Linked Model to a Host Project

1. In the *Insert* tab>Link panel, click 🄬 (Link Revit).
2. In the Import/Link RVT dialog box, select the file that you want to link. Before opening the file, set the *Positioning*, as shown in Figure 1–12.

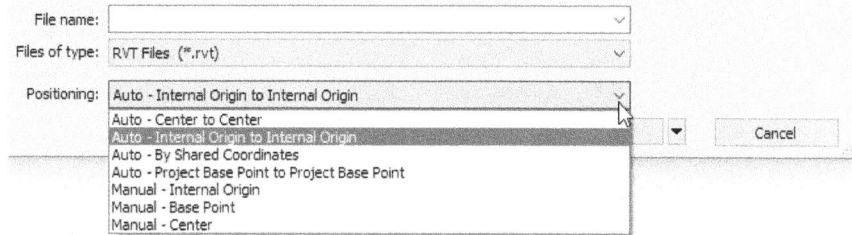

File name:	
Files of type:	RVT Files (*.rvt)
Positioning:	Auto - Internal Origin to Internal Origin

Auto - Center to Center
Auto - Internal Origin to Internal Origin
Auto - By Shared Coordinates
Auto - Project Base Point to Project Base Point
Manual - Internal Origin
Manual - Base Point
Manual - Center

Cancel

Figure 1–12

3. Click **Open**.

• Depending on how you decide to position the file, either it is automatically placed in the project or you can manually place it with the cursor.

How To: Link a CAD File

1. Open the view into which you want to link or import the file.
   • For a 2D file, this should be a 2D view. For a 3D file, open a 3D view.

2. In the *Insert* tab>Link panel, click 🗎 (Link CAD), or in the *Insert* tab>Import panel, click 🗎 (Import CAD).

3. In the Link CAD Formats or Import CAD Formats dialog box (shown in Figure 1–13), select the file that you want to import.

- Select a file format in the Files of type drop-down list to limit the files that are displayed.

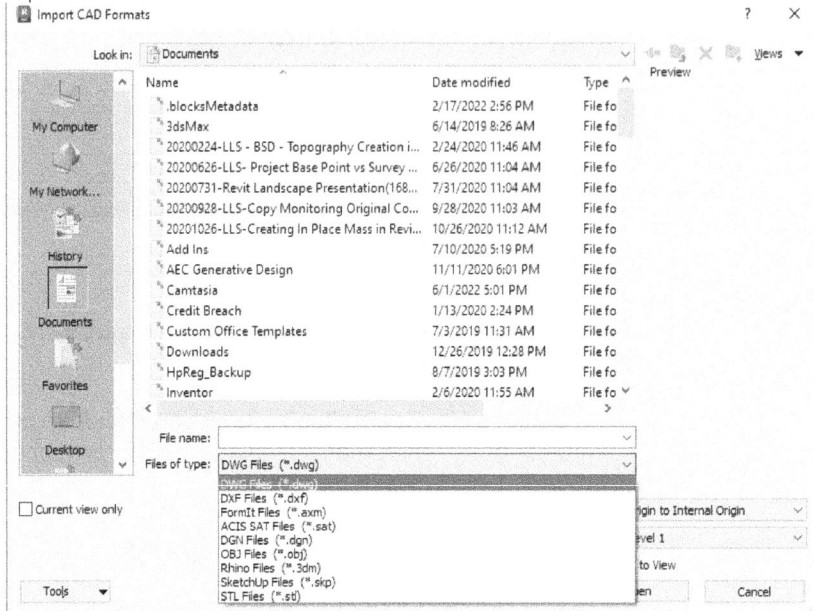

Figure 1–13

4. Set the other options and the *Positioning* (as shown in Figure 1–14) as specified by your office standards. The table below describes these settings in more detail.

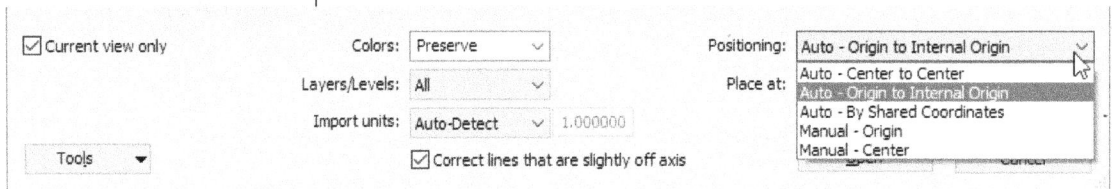

Figure 1–14

5. Click **Open**.

CAD Linking Options

Current view only	This option determines whether the CAD file is placed in every view, or only in the current view. Turn this option off if you are linking a topography from a CAD file so you can see it in a 3D view as well.
Colors	Specify the color settings. Typically, Revit projects are black and white; however, other software frequently uses color. You can **Invert** the original colors, **Preserve** them, or change everything to **Black and White**.
Layers/ Levels	Indicate which CAD layers are going to be brought into the model. Select how you want layers to be imported: **All**, **Visible**, or **Specify....**
Import units	Select the units of the original file, as required. **Auto-Detect** works in most cases.
Correct lines...	If lines in a CAD file are off axis by less than 0.1 degrees, selecting this option straightens them. It is selected by default.
Positioning	Specify how you want the linked file to be positioned in the current project: **Auto - Center to Center, Auto - Origin to Internal Origin, Auto - By Shared Coordinates, Manual - Origin**, or **Manual - Center**. They follow the same principles as described in the Link Positioning Options table above.
Place at	Select a level in which to place the imported file. If you selected **Current view only**, this option is grayed out.
Orient to View	Used to orient the CAD file on import/link.

Hint: Preventing a Linked Model from Being Moved

Once a linked model is in the correct location, you can lock it in place to ensure it does not get moved by mistake or to prevent the linked model from being selected.

- To pin the linked model in place, select it and in the *Modify* tab>Modify panel, click ⬚ (Pin).
- To prevent pinned elements from being selected, in the Status Bar, click ⬚ (Select Pinned Elements).
- To toggle off the ability to select links, in the Status Bar, click ⬚ (Select Links).

If a linked model is moved, you can reposition it to the project base point or internal origin. Right-click on the model and select the appropriate option, as shown in Figure 1–15.

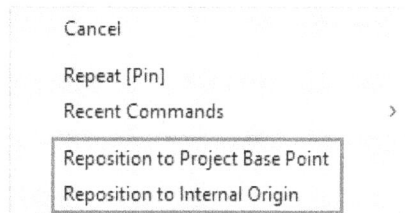

Cancel

Repeat [Pin]

Recent Commands   >

Reposition to Project Base Point
Reposition to Internal Origin

Figure 1–15

Multiple Linked Models or Copies of Linked Models

Copied instances of a linked model are typically used when creating a master project with the same building placed in multiple locations, such as a university campus with six identical student residence halls.

- Within the host model, you can display linked model coordinates by turning them on from the Visibility/Graphic Overrides dialog box, in the Site category. Linked model coordinates will be grayed out in the view, as shown in Figure 1–16.

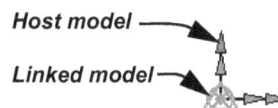

Host model

Linked model

Figure 1–16

- Linked models can be moved, copied, rotated, arrayed, and mirrored. There is only one linked model, and any copies are additional instances of the link.

- Copies are numbered automatically. You can change their names in Properties when the instance is selected.

- When you have placed a link in a project, you can drag and drop additional copies of the link into the project from the Project Browser>**Revit Links** node, as shown in Figure 1–17.

Figure 1–17

Hint: Working with Civil 3D Files

If the project is being coordinated in BIM 360, the civil engineer can publish surfaces to BIM 360 Documents. The surface can be brought into Revit from the *Insert* tab>Link panel by clicking

(Link Topography).

If the coordinates have already been acquired, the topography will place itself in the correct location based on those coordinates. Since the file is linked into the project, when the civil engineer updates the file, it will also update accordingly inside the Revit project.

Managing Links

The Manage Links dialog box (shown in Figure 1–18) enables you to reload, unload, add, and remove links. It also provides access to set other options. To open the Manage Links dialog box, in the *Insert* tab>Link panel, click 📑 (Manage Links). Alternatively, you can go to the *Manage* tab>Manage Projects panel and click 📑 (Manage Links).

- You can also select the link and click 📑 (Manage Links) in the *Modify | RVT Links* tab>Link panel.

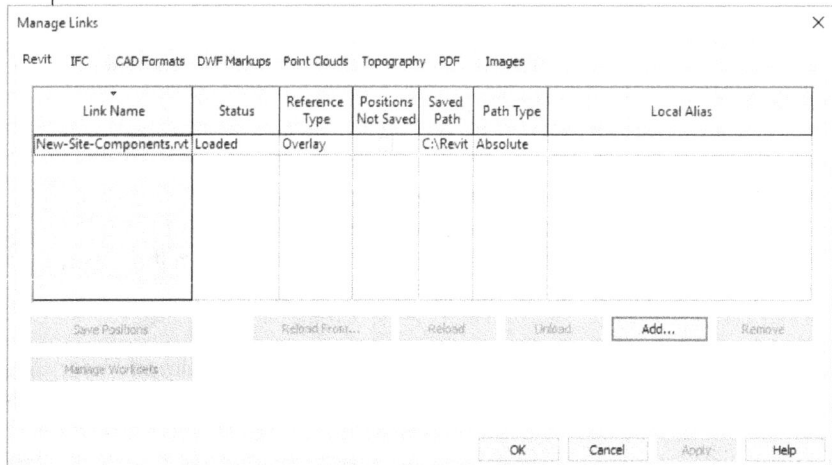

Figure 1–18

The options available include the following:

*Some of these options are also available in the Project Browser. Expand the Revit Links node, then right-click on the Revit link and select **Reload, Unload**, or **Reload From...**.*

- **Reload From...:** Opens the Add Link dialog box, which enables you to select the file you want to reload. Use this if the linked file location or name has changed.
- **Reload:** Reloads the file without additional prompts.
- **Unload:** Unloads the file so that the link is kept, but the file is not displayed or calculated in the project. Use **Reload** to restore it.
- **Add:** Opens the Import/Link RVT dialog box, which enables you to link additional models into the host project.
- **Remove:** Deletes the link from the file.

Links can be nested into one another. How a link responds when the host project is linked into another project depends on the option selected in the *Reference Type* column:

- **Overlay:** The nested linked model is not referenced in the new host project.

- **Attach:** The nested linked model displays in the new host project.

The option in the *Path Type* column controls how the location of the link is remembered:

- **Relative:** Searches for the link in the root folder of the current project. If the file is moved, the software still searches for it.

- **Absolute:** Searches the entire file path where the file was originally saved. If the original file is moved, the software is not able to find it.

Other options control how the linked file interfaces with worksets and shared positioning.

Reposition Linked Revit Models

Regardless of how a Revit model was linked into the host project, you have two options to reposition the linked model after insertion: **Reposition to Internal Origin** (as shown in Figure 1–19), which aligns the linked model's internal origin with the host model's origin, and **Reposition to Project Base Point**, which aligns the linked model's project base point with the host model's project base point.

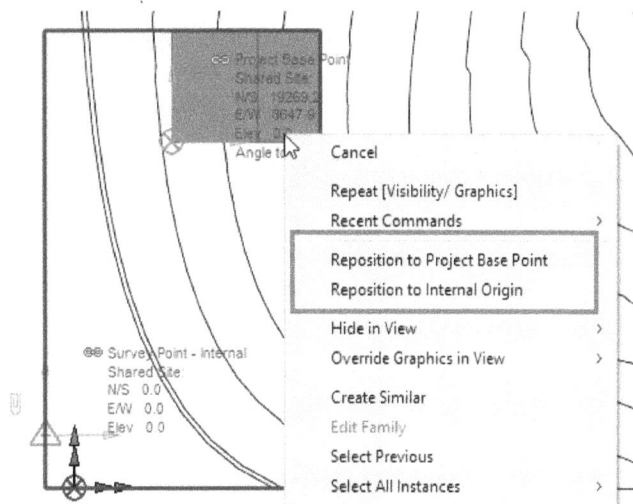

Figure 1–19

If a linked instance has been rotated or mirrored and you select one of the reposition options, you will be asked if you want to preserve the orientation of the linked model or reset the orientation, which re-aligns it to its original position (as shown in Figure 1–20).

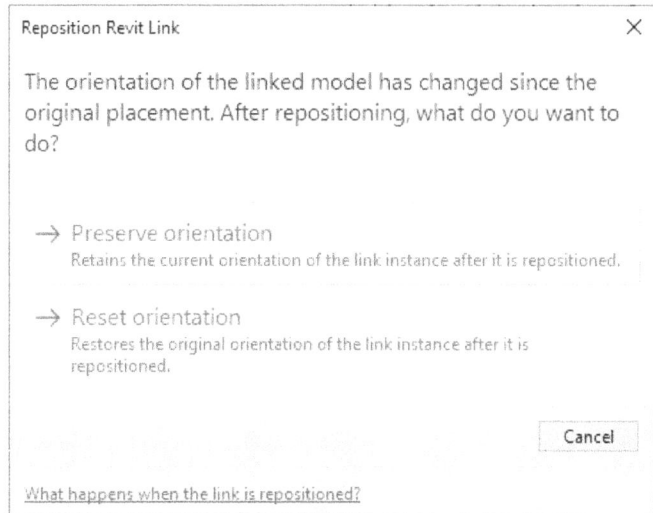

Reposition Revit Link ✕

The orientation of the linked model has changed since the original placement. After repositioning, what do you want to do?

→ Preserve orientation
Retains the current orientation of the link instance after it is repositioned.

→ Reset orientation
Restores the original orientation of the link instance after it is repositioned.

Cancel

What happens when the link is repositioned?

Figure 1–20

Relocate the Project

After you have linked in the site plan or linked a model into your site plan, you need to make sure you have lined up the project and site plan so that when you are working in a plan, elevation, or section view, everything is in the right location. You can use the Align and Move tools to get the link into position. There are also tools you can use to move the model elements without physically moving them. As well, you can specify whether the levels will read the project base point or survey point.

- The **Relocate Project** tool is used to relocate the project to the correct position of a linked file without physically moving the elements in a project. An example of why you would want to use the Relocate Project tool is if, in plan view, your survey point is in the correct position but your project base point is off and you need to move your building to the correct location. In elevation view, you would want to use the Relocate Project tool if your model is not at the correct elevation location and you need to move it into position.

- **Specify Coordinates at Point** is used when you have the coordinates from a civil engineer or surveyor, or if you have a linked model in your Revit host model and you use the Report Shared Coordinates tool to determine the coordinates of the linked model. This tool allows you to enter values for *North/South*, *East/West*, *Elevation*, and *Angle from Project North to True North*, as shown in Figure 1–21.

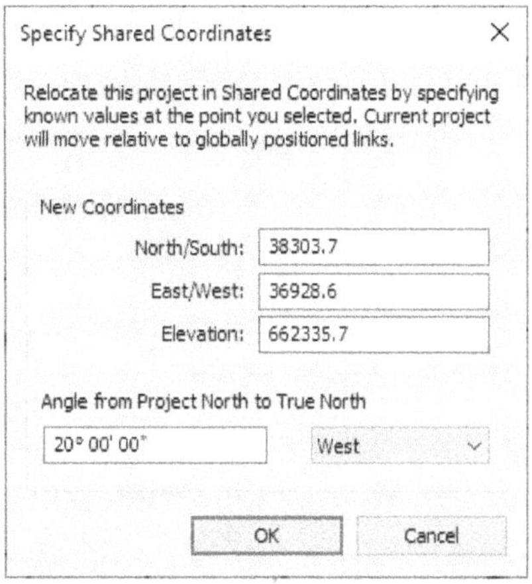

Figure 1–21

Hint: When to Relocate the Host Model

In a common workflow, repositioning the host model relative to your survey point may be required in any of the following situations:

- If you are given the survey point location from the civil engineer or surveyor and you want to align your building model and levels to the given coordinates.

- If after linking in your site plan, you need to line up your building with the site.

- After acquiring a site plan's coordinates and linking in files or models and publishing coordinates.

How To: Relocate the Model Using Relocate Project

1. In a plan or elevation view, in the *Manage* tab>Project Location panel, expand 🏠 (Position) and select

   ↳⁺ (Relocate Project).
2. Select somewhere within the view as the starting base point. The second point selected is where you want to move the model to. Use the temporary dimensions to enter a precise distance.

How To: Relocate the Model by Specifying Coordinates

1. In a plan or elevation view, in the *Manage* tab>Project Location panel, expand ↳ (Coordinates) and select

   ↳¹,² (Specify Coordinates at Point).
2. Select somewhere within the view as the starting base point.
3. In the Specify Shared Coordinates dialog box, enter the coordinates given to you by the surveyor or civil engineer.

Adjust the Levels' Elevation Base

In an elevation view, you can set your levels to read the project base point or survey point. Changing this allows you to measure based off of the sea level elevation (provided the correct shared coordinates are set up) without physically moving your model.

How To: Change the Levels' Elevation Base

1. In an elevation view, select a level.
2. In Properties, click **Edit Type**. In the Type Properties dialog box, in the *Constraints* section, change the *Elevation Base* to **Survey Point**, as shown in Figure 1–22. Note the difference in the levels once the *Elevation Base* has been changed.

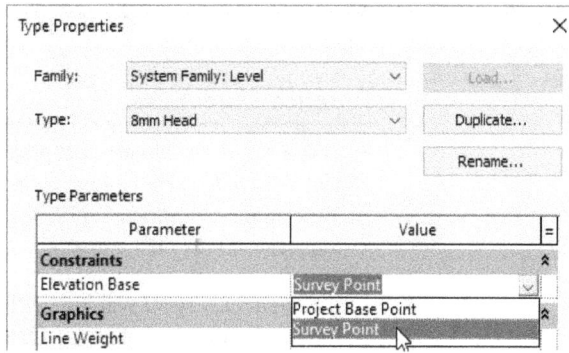

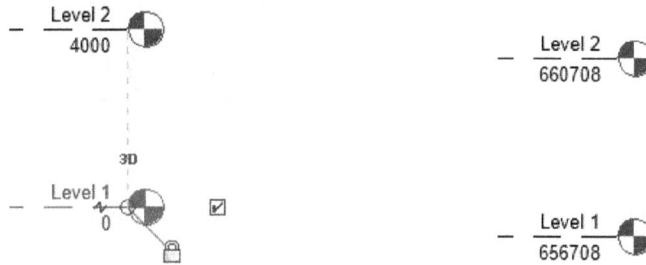

Elevation Base set to Project Base Point   Elevation Base set to Survey Point

Figure 1–22

Practice 1a | Link and Modify Positioning

Practice Objectives

- Link a .DWG file into the host project.
- Link a Revit file into the host project.
- Test different locations.
- Manually set the host project's survey point.

In this practice, you will link a file to a host project using **Auto - Internal Origin to Internal Origin** and **Auto - Project Base Point to Project Base Point**, demonstrating what happens when you use the different positioning methods (shown in Figure 1–23) available in the Link dialog box. You will also learn how to reposition a model after it is linked in. Finally, you will manually set the survey point on the site plan.

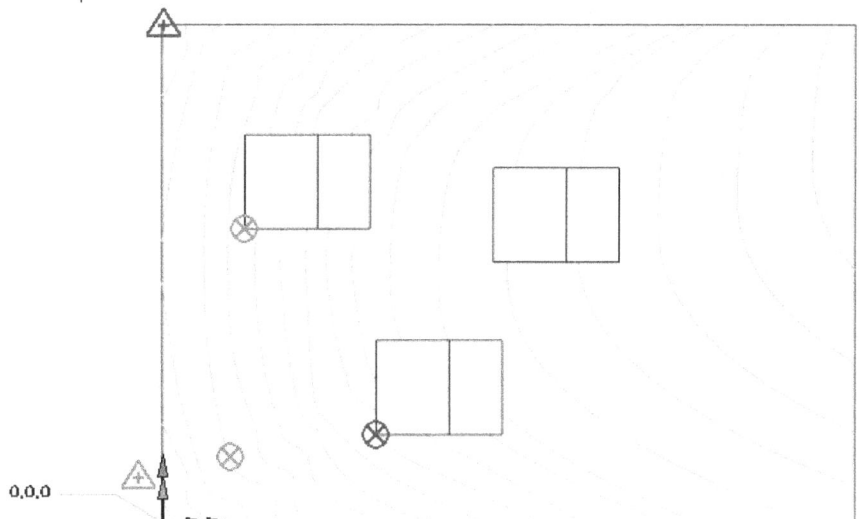

Figure 1–23

Task 1 - Link the CAD site plan.

In this task, you will link a .DWG file into your project. Its coordinates (0,0,0) are located in the bottom left of the drawing and are marked with a leader line.

1. In the practice files folder, open **Host Model-M.rvt**. You should be on the **Floor Plans: Site** view.

2. In the *Insert* tab>Link panel, click ⬛ (Link CAD).

3. In the Link CAD Formats dialog box, navigate to the practice files *CAD* folder and select **BCM_Site Plan-M.dwg**. Set the *Positioning* to **Auto - Origin to Internal Origin** and leave the defaults as shown in Figure 1–24. Click **Open**.

☐ Current view only	Colors: Preserve ⌄	Positioning: Auto - Origin to Internal Origin ⌄
	Layers/Levels: All ⌄	Place at: Level 1 ⌄
	Import units: Auto-Detect ⌄ 1.000000	☑ Orient to View
Tools ▼	☑ Correct lines that are slightly off axis	Open Cancel

Figure 1–24

• You will note that the .DWG file's coordinates (0,0,0) line up with Revit's internal origin (0,0,0), as shown in Figure 1–25.

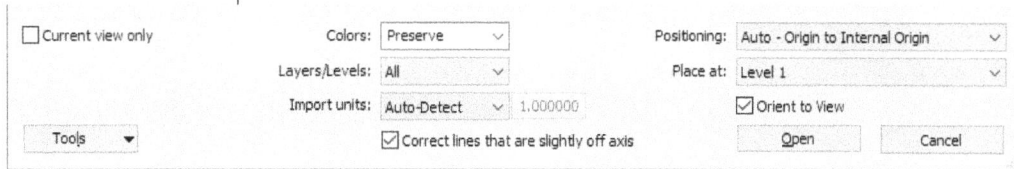

.DWG's 0,0,0 origin

0,0,0

Revit's internal origin

Figure 1–25

Task 2 - Link the Revit building model.

In this task, you will link in a Revit building to see how it will line up with the host model. Because the site internal origin and survey and project base point icons are turned on, you will also see the linked model's site icons but they will be grayed out.

1. In the *Insert* tab>Link panel, click 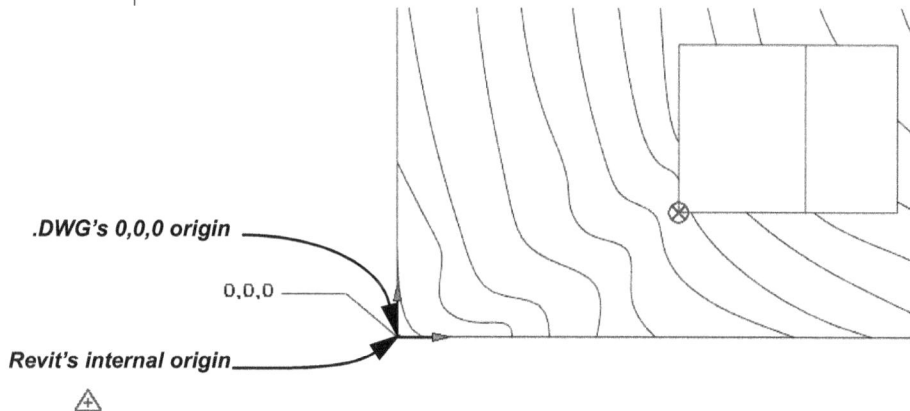 (Link Revit).

2. In the Import/Link RVT dialog box, navigate to the practice files folder and select **Building-M.rvt**. Set the *Positioning* to **Auto - Internal Origin to Internal Origin** and click **Open**.

3. You will see that the linked .RVT file's internal origin is lined up with the host model's internal origin, as shown in Figure 1–26. (The linked model's internal origin is grayed out.)

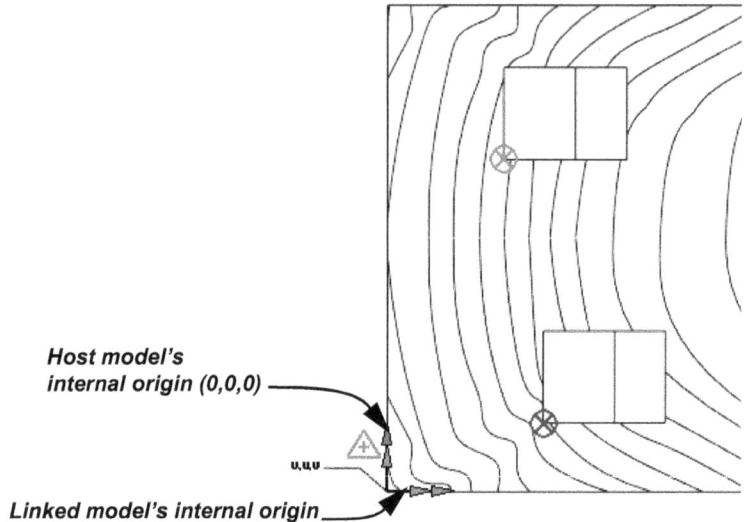

Figure 1–26

4. In the *Insert* tab>Link panel, click (Link Revit).

5. In the Import/Link RVT dialog box, navigate to the practice files folder and select **Annex-M.rvt**. Set the *Positioning* to **Auto - Project Base Point to Project Base Point** and click **Open**.

• You will note that the host model's project base point and the linked Annex-M.rvt's project base point are now lined up and on top of each other, as shown in Figure 1–27.

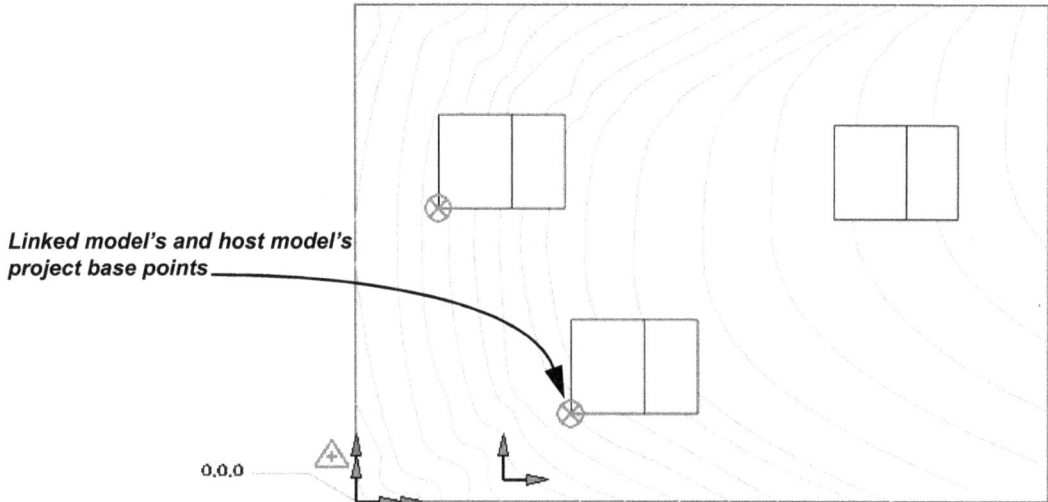

Linked model's and host model's project base points

0,0,0

Figure 1–27

Task 3 - Move the annex to a new position.

1. In the view, select the linked **Annex-M.rvt** model, right-click, and select **Reposition to Internal Origin**, as shown in Figure 1–28.

   - The linked annex building's internal origin now aligns with the host model's internal origin.

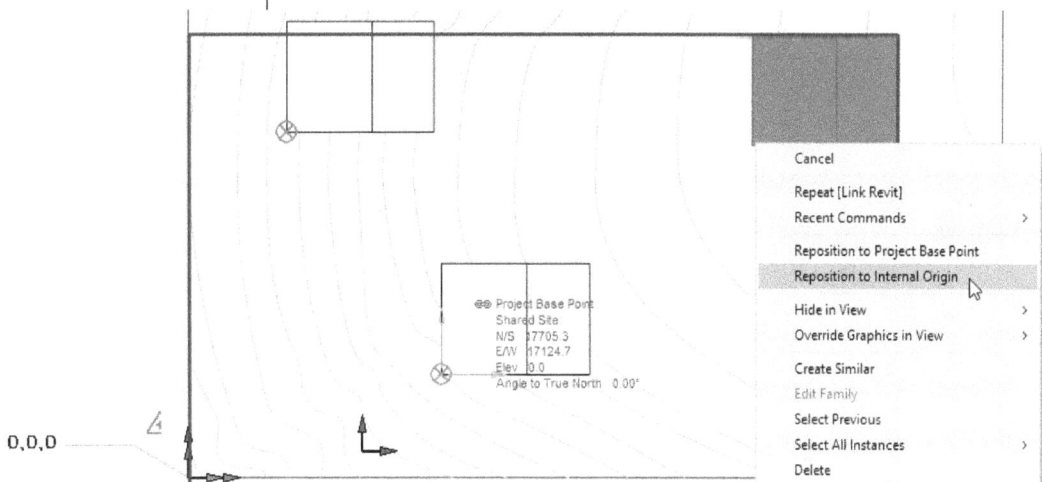

Cancel

Repeat [Link Revit]
Recent Commands

Reposition to Project Base Point
Reposition to Internal Origin

Hide in View
Override Graphics in View

Create Similar
Edit Family
Select Previous
Select All Instances
Delete

Project Base Point
Shared Site
N/S 37705.3
E/W 17124.7
Elev 0.0
Angle to True North 0.00°

0,0,0

Figure 1–28

Task 4 - Manually set the host model's survey point.

In this task, you will unclip the survey point and enter in the coordinates in Properties. Note that this is the approach you would take to set up your host model for real-world coordinates given by the surveyor.

1. In the view, select the survey point and click 📎 (Change clip state of point) to unclip it, as shown in Figure 1–29. Note that *N/S*, *E/W*, and *Elev* are now editable in Properties.

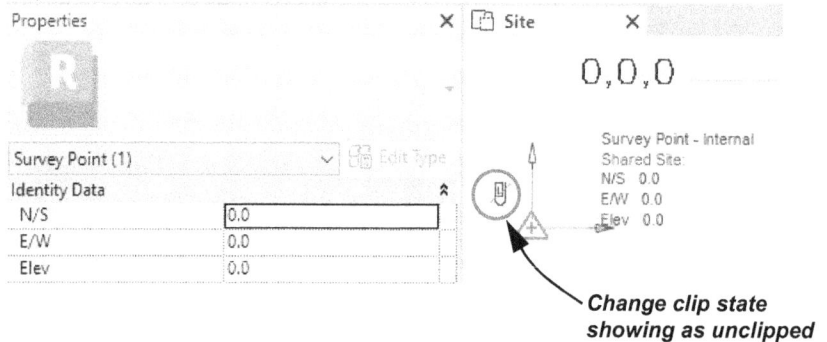

Change clip state showing as unclipped

Figure 1–29

2. In Properties, enter the following:

   - *N/S*: **41468.4**
   - *E/W:* **13888.6**
   - *Elev*: **0.0**

3. The survey point is now located in the upper left corner of the site plan. Select the survey point and click 📎 (Change clip state of point) to clip it, as shown in Figure 1–30.

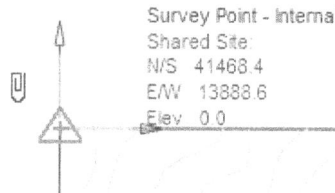

Figure 1–30

Task 5 - Manually move the survey point in a clipped state.

1. Select the survey point and click ⬄ (Change clip state of point) to unclip it. In Properties, change both *N/S* and *E/W* back to **0.0**. This places the survey point back to its original location/position.

2. Select the survey point and click ⬄ (Change clip state of point) to clip it.

    •   Note that a similar approach can be taken if the survey point has been moved to real-world coordinates. Changing the point's state to clipped allows the survey point to be moved from really far away (e.g., 1500 N/S and 1500 E/W) from the internal origin back closer to the origin point so that the model does not exceed the 16km radius limit.

3. Keeping the survey point clipped, manually move the survey point to the upper corner of the site plan. Note that the survey point still shows as **0,0,0**, as shown in Figure 1–31.

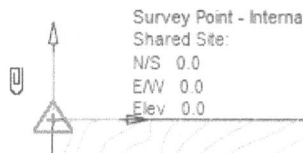

Figure 1–31

4. Save and close the project.

1.4 Shared Coordinates

Shared coordinates are used to maintain the relationship between the host model and all linked files associated with it. **Publish Coordinates** and **Acquire Coordinates** are two ways to activate shared coordinates after files and models have been linked into your host model. You will use the method that is established by your BIM manager. Note that you cannot publish or acquire coordinates from an imported file.

The following are some examples of when you would use one of these methods.

- If you are working in a project with linked models and want to adopt the coordinates from one of the linked models, rather than from the host project, you can acquire the coordinates, as shown in Figure 1–32. For example, you might have a site plan that was created in AutoCAD that has been linked into your Revit project and you want to use the coordinates from the AutoCAD .DWG file.

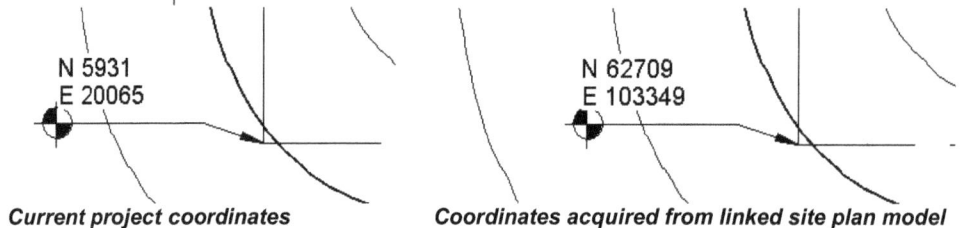

N 5931
E 20065

Current project coordinates

N 62709
E 103349

Coordinates acquired from linked site plan model

Figure 1–32

- If you are working in a project with linked models and want the linked models to adopt your coordinates, you would publish your coordinates to them. Publishing coordinates is also used when you are linking or copying more than one file or model.

  - For example, you might have a project that has multiple buildings, like a campus, or multiple rooms that are the same, like an apartment complex (as shown in Figure 1–33). You can define unique positions for each of the copied linked models by specifying a named position through the link's instance properties.

- If working with models that are within your own office on the same network, it is best practice to not have anyone working in the linked file when you publish coordinates to it.

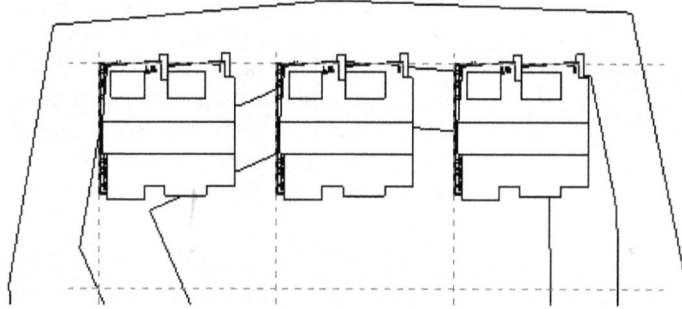

Figure 1–33

Hint: Geographic Location Information

To maintain a consistent geographic location (geolocation) between models, you can use the Geographic Information System (GIS) coordinates stored in a linked .DWG file that includes a geographic marker, as shown in the AutoCAD software in Figure 1–34. The geolocation is a specific real-world location using global coordinates.

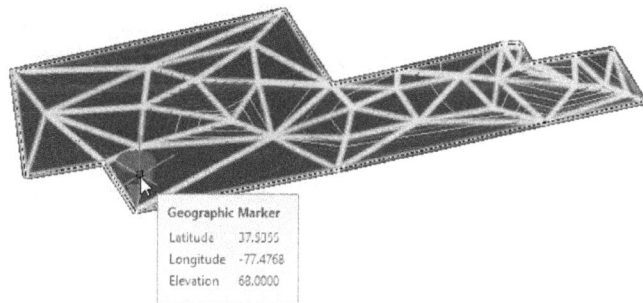

Geographic Marker	
Latitude	37.5055
Longitude	-77.4768
Elevation	68.0000

Figure 1–34

When you acquire coordinates from a geographic marker (as shown in Figure 1–35), this updates the Revit model with the real-world position of the model, which improves energy analysis.

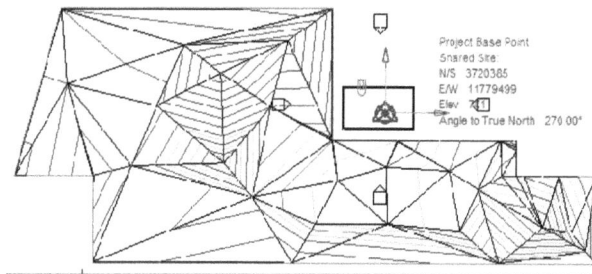

Project Base Point
Shared Site:
N/S 3720385
E/W 11779499
Elev 7[ ]
Angle to True North 276.00°

Figure 1–35

Acquire Coordinates

Acquiring coordinates is adopting or pulling coordinates from a single linked model, typically from a site plan. This could be a CAD file or a linked Revit model. There are two ways that you can acquire coordinates from a linked model: use the tools from the *Manage* tab>Project Location panel or use the linked file's instance properties to select the *Shared Site* parameter and bring up the Share Coordinates dialog box.

- If you are working with a linked site, before acquiring the coordinates, ensure that you move, rotate, and align your model into place.

- Linked models that share coordinates can be a combination of file types like .RVT, .DWG, and .DXF.

- You can only acquire coordinates once.

How To: Acquire Coordinates from a Linked File or Model

1. In the *Manage* tab>Project Location panel, expand ⌞ (Coordinates) and click ⌞ (Acquire Coordinates).
2. Select a linked model from which to acquire the shared coordinate system.
   - You will get an Acquire Coordinates Succeed dialog box specifying the name of the file you acquired from, as shown in Figure 1–36 for both a .DWG file and a .RVT file.

Acquire Coordinates Succeed ✕

Coordinates acquired from CAD Site Contours.dwg.

GIS Coordinate System: UTM-WGS 1984 datum, Zone 18 North, Meter; Cent. Meridian 75d W

Close

Acquire Coordinates Succeed ✕

Coordinates acquired from New-Site-Modify_CB.rvt.

GIS Coordinate System: <Unknown>

Close

Figure 1–36

- The current project now uses the new coordinates.

How To: Acquire Coordinates Using Instance Properties

1. In your project, select the linked file or model.
2. In Properties, in the *Other* section, beside *Shared Site,* click **<Not Shared>**, as shown in Figure 1–37.

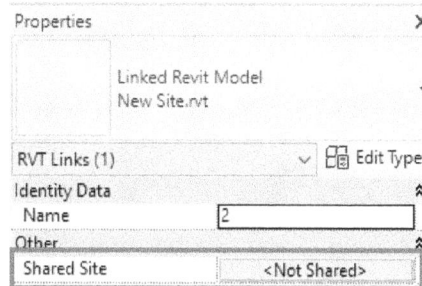

Figure 1–37

3. In the Share Coordinates dialog box, select the **Acquire** option and click **Reconcile**, as shown in Figure 1–38.

   • You will not have this option if you select an imported file.

Figure 1–38

   • This only occurs the first time you select a file that does not share coordinates. If you select other instances of the same link, this dialog box does not open. Instead, you will get the Choose Site dialog box.

- If you move or rotate a linked instance after it has been shared and saved, a Warning box displays, as shown in Figure 1–39. You can click **Save Now** to save the position or click **OK** to continue working in the project. You can save the linked model later using the Manage Links dialog box.

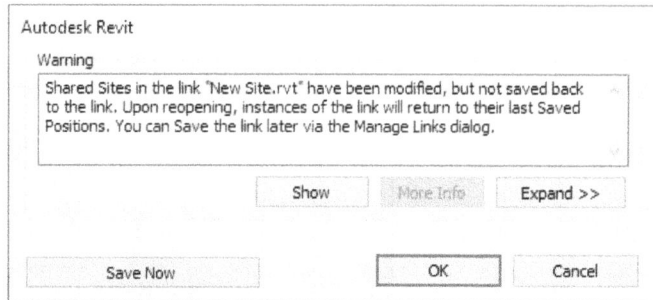

Autodesk Revit

Warning

Shared Sites in the link "New Site.rvt" have been modified, but not saved back to the link. Upon reopening, instances of the link will return to their last Saved Positions. You can Save the link later via the Manage Links dialog.

Show   More Info   Expand >>

Save Now   OK   Cancel

Figure 1–39

Hint: Project North and True North

When you acquire coordinates, they include the orientation of the site. When you are working on a building or site layout, it is easier to work with standard horizontal and vertical axes, as shown on the left in Figure 1–40. This is called project north. You can also display a view at true north, as shown on the right in Figure 1–40.

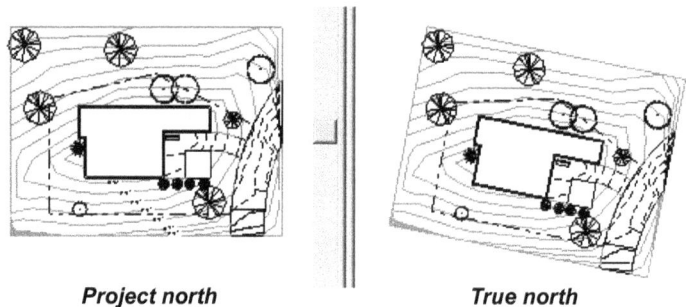

Project north   *True north*

Figure 1–40

- To change the orientation, activate the view where you want to change the orientation. With no elements selected, in Properties, in the *Graphics* section, set the *Orientation* to **True North**.

Publish Coordinates

Publishing coordinates is pushing the host model's coordinates to a linked file or model. This could be a CAD file or a linked Revit model. This is typically done when the Revit host model has already been given the survey coordinates from the civil engineer or surveyor and they have been manually entered as the host model's survey point. There are two ways that you can publish coordinates from a linked model: use the tools from the *Manage* tab>Project Location panel or use the linked file's instance properties to select the *Shared Site* parameter and bring up the Share Coordinates dialog box.

- You can publish coordinates to more than one linked file or model. This ensures that all files that are linked in are using the same coordinate system.

How To: Publish Coordinates to a Linked File or Model

1. Ensure you are in the host project that has the coordinates you want to push or publish to the linked model.
2. In the *Manage* tab>Project Location panel, expand

   (Coordinates) and click (Publish Coordinates).
3. Select the linked model you want to publish the coordinates to.

How To: Publish Coordinates Using Instance Properties

1. In your project, select the linked file or model.
2. In Properties, in the *Other* section, beside *Shared Site,* click **<Not Shared>**, as shown in Figure 1–41.

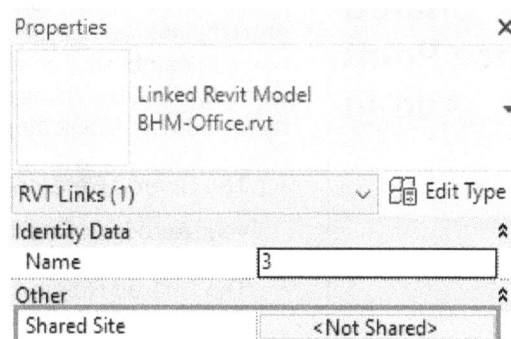

Figure 1–41

3. In the Share Coordinates dialog box, select the **Publish** option and click **Reconcile**, as shown in Figure 1–42.

   • You will not have this option if you select an imported file.

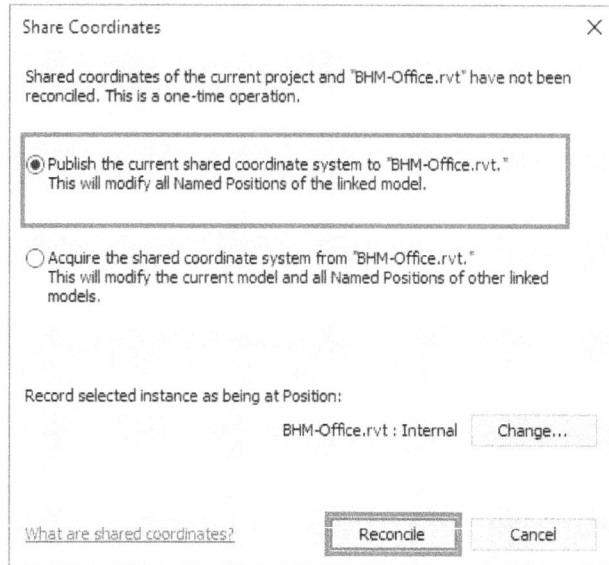

Figure 1–42

• You only need to publish coordinates to a linked model once.

• The Share Coordinates dialog box only displays the first time you select a linked model or file that does not share coordinates. If you select other instances of the same link, this dialog box does not open. Instead, you will get the Choose Site dialog box.

Shared Reference Point Add-In

As an alternative to using a linked-in file to establish your project's shared coordinates, there is an Autodesk add-in that helps to establish a shared coordinate system within Revit when working with files created in Autodesk Civil 3D, allowing you to bypass the previous steps outlined above.

• The Shared Reference Point extension can be installed from your Autodesk Desktop App ().

• The Shared Reference Point extension is for Autodesk Subscription customers only.

• There are two downloads: one for Civil 3D and one for Revit.

• The shared coordinate file needs to be created in Civil 3D before it can be imported into Revit.

How To: Import Shared Reference Points from Civil 3D

1. In the *Add-Ins* tab>Shared Reference Point panel, click **Import Shared Coordinates from XML file**.
2. Select the two points to align to: the origin point and the point on the +Y (up) direction (quasi-north) that were established in the Civil 3D file. You may need to verify these two points with the civil engineer or surveyor. The order of the selected points is important.
3. In the Open dialog box, navigate to the XML file that was created in Civil 3D. Select the file and click **Open**.
4. In the User Confirmation dialog box (shown in Figure 1–43), click **Yes** to confirm that you want to create a new shared coordinate. A new site is being created for this coordinate system.

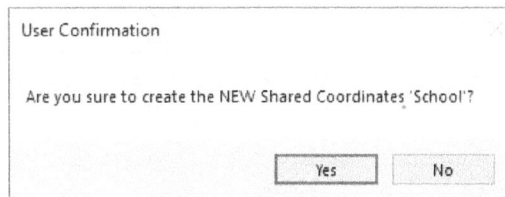

User Confirmation

Are you sure to create the NEW Shared Coordinates 'School'?

Yes   No

Figure 1–43

5. In the dialog box that displays to let you know it was successfully set, click **OK**.
6. Next, you need to set your project's location to the XML file. In the *Manage* tab>Project Location panel, click

    (Location).
7. In the Location and Site dialog box, select the *Site* tab.
8. In the *Sites defined in this project* area, select the name of the XML file (as shown in Figure 1–44) and select **Make Current**, then click **OK**.

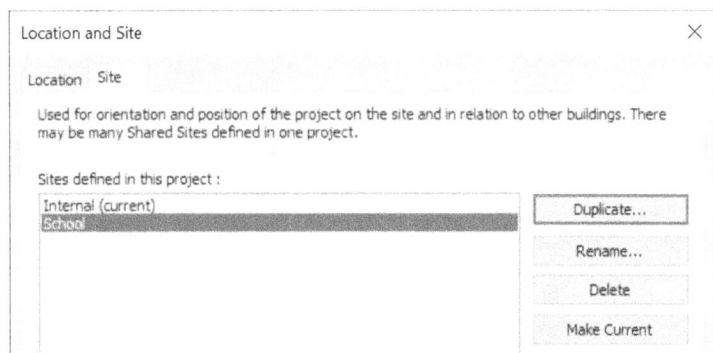

Location and Site   ×

Location   Site

Used for orientation and position of the project on the site and in relation to other buildings. There may be many Shared Sites defined in one project.

Sites defined in this project :

Internal (current)	Duplicate...
School	Rename...
	Delete
	Make Current

Figure 1–44

- Your project is now utilizing the shared coordinates from the Civil 3D XML file and you are ready to link in the DWG site plan that created the XML file.

How To: Link the DWG Site File That Created the XML File

1. In the Site plan view, click 🗎 (Link CAD) in the *Insert* tab>Link panel.
2. In the Link CAD Formats dialog box, select the file that you want to import.
3. Set the options as follows (as shown in Figure 1–45) to ensure accuracy:
   - Uncheck **Correct lines that are slightly off axis** and **Orient to View** so Revit does not try to correct the drawing.
   - Set the *Positioning* to **Auto - By Shared Coordinates**.
   - Set the *Import units* to match the .DWG file given to you by the surveyor or civil engineer.

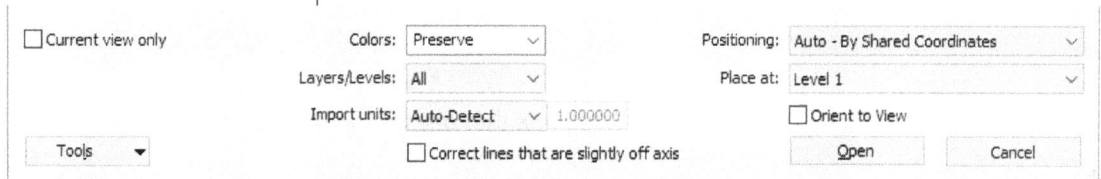

☐ Current view only	Colors: Preserve ⌄	Positioning: Auto - By Shared Coordinates ⌄
	Layers/Levels: All ⌄	Place at: Level 1 ⌄
	Import units: Auto-Detect ⌄ 1.000000	☐ Orient to View
Tools ▼	☐ Correct lines that are slightly off axis	Open Cancel

Figure 1–45

4. Click **Open**. The .DWG file will be inserted into the project based on the XML's shared coordinates.

Define Named Positions

When you have more than one unique building or multiple copies of a building linked into the host model, you can specify their positions on a site through the linked file's instance properties. This is done by selecting the link in the view and modifying the *Shared Site* parameter, which is located in the *Other* section in Properties, as shown in Figure 1–46. Through Properties, you can move a linked instance to a new location, record the current position to a named location, or stop sharing the location of the linked instance.

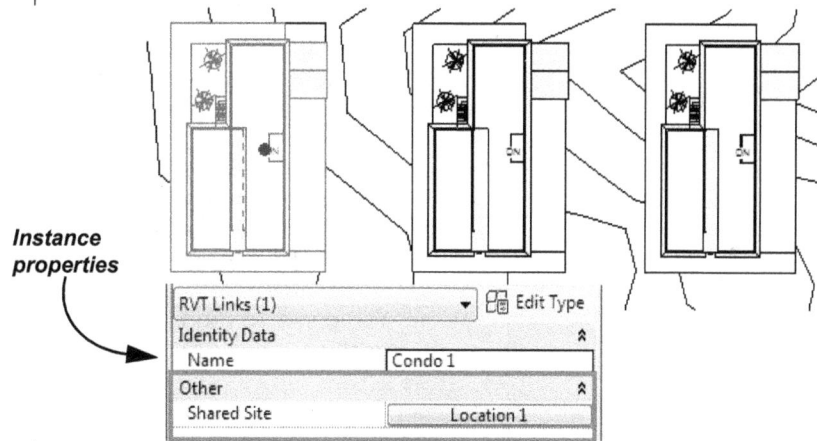

Instance properties

Figure 1–46

Once you click the button next to the *Shared Site* parameter, the Choose Site dialog box displays. You have the option to do one of the following:

- **Move instance to:** You can move the linked instance to a named position that is specified within the linked model.
- **Record current position as:** You can record the current position of the linked model where you have positioned it in the host model. This saves the position back to the linked model.
- **Do not share site of selected instance:** Selecting this option leaves the linked model's position in its original position from when it was first linked in. Use this option to move the linked model without modifying the linked model's position. The linked model's *Shared Site* parameter will display as **<Not Shared>**.

If you have selected the option to **Record current position as** and click the **Change...** button, the Location and Site dialog box displays, where you can choose from the list of positions or duplicate and name a new position.

- The default named position is called **Internal** and its position is set to Revit's internal origin. In the Location and Site dialog box (shown in Figure 1–47), you can delete, rename, and duplicate defined positions in a project.

  - You can also rename the default **Internal (current)** position.

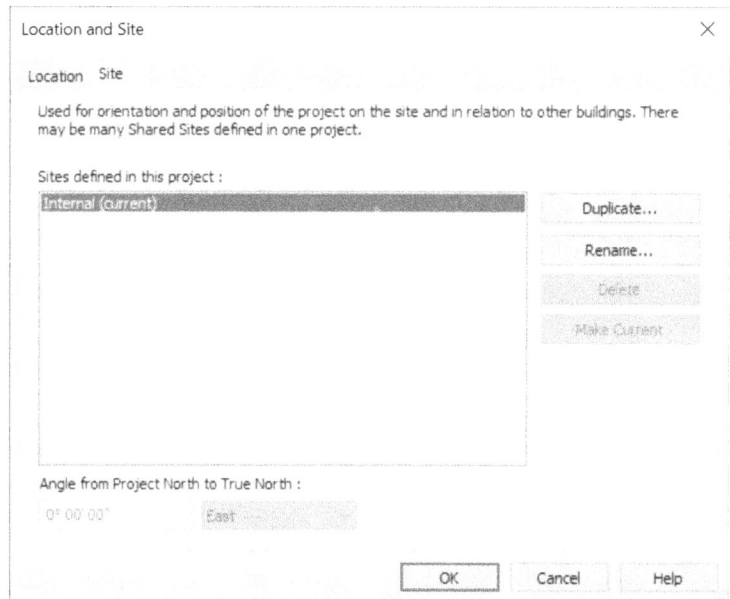

Figure 1–47

When you have specified the positioning of the linked models and you save the host model, if you have not saved the recorded positions through the Manage Links dialog box, you are prompted with the Location Position Changed dialog box, letting you know that you have changed a position of a linked model and prompting if you want to **Save**, **Do not save**, or **Disable shared positioning**, as shown in Figure 1–48.

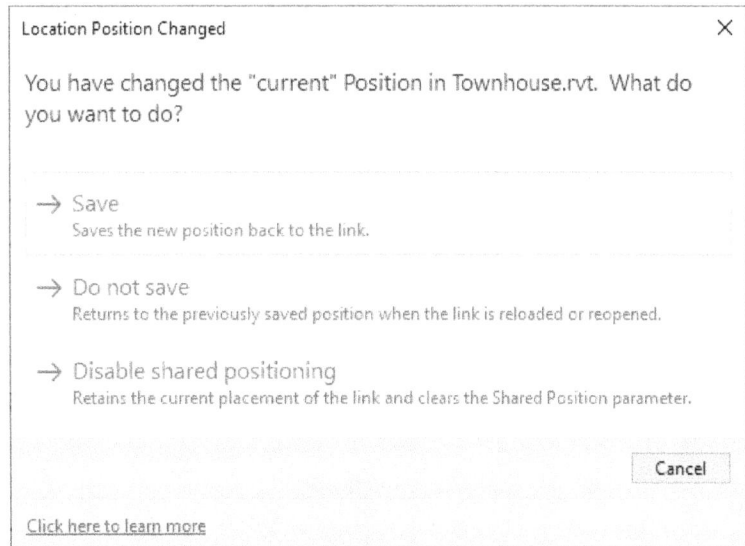

Figure 1–48

How To: Change or Record a Position Using Instance Properties

1. Select a linked file that you want to change or record the position of in the host model.
2. In Properties, in the *Other* section, click the button beside *Shared Site*.
3. The Choose Site dialog box opens. Click **Change...**, as shown in Figure 1–49.

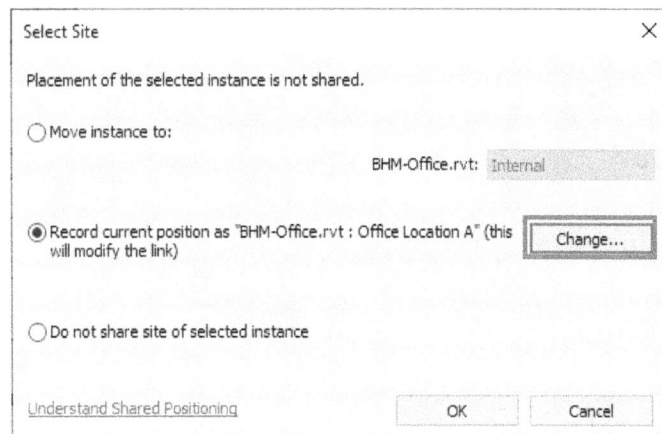

Figure 1–49

4. In the Location and Site dialog box, verify that you are on the *Site* tab, as shown in Figure 1–50.

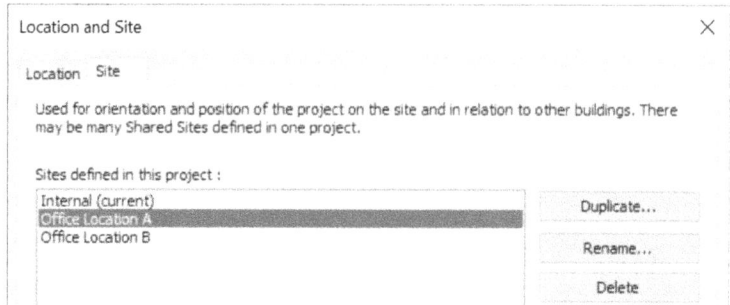

Click ⊕ (Location) in the Manage tab>Project Location panel to open the dialog box at any time.

Location and Site ✕

Location Site

Used for orientation and position of the project on the site and in relation to other buildings. There may be many Shared Sites defined in one project.

Sites defined in this project :

Internal (current)	Duplicate...
Office Location A	
Office Location B	Rename...
	Delete

Figure 1–50

- The **Internal** named location of the linked model is the default.

  - Click **Rename...** to give the default location a different name.
  - Click **Duplicate...** to create a new name for the instance location. Each instance of the linked model should have a differently named location.

5. Select the location that you want to use and click **OK** twice.
6. The value of the *Shared Site* option is now the new location name, as shown in Figure 1–51. You can also specify a name for the linked model in the *Identity Data* section.

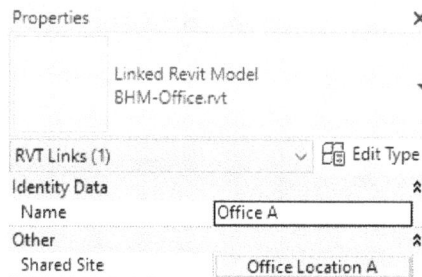

Properties ✕

Linked Revit Model
BHM-Office.rvt

RVT Links (1) ⊟ Edit Type

Identity Data ⌃
  Name   Office A
Other ⌃
  Shared Site   Office Location A

Figure 1–51

Multiple Linked Copies

If you have copies of the same linked file or model in the host project and you select another instance of the same link, the Share Coordinates dialog box does not open. Instead, you will get the Choose Site dialog box, as shown in Figure 1–52.

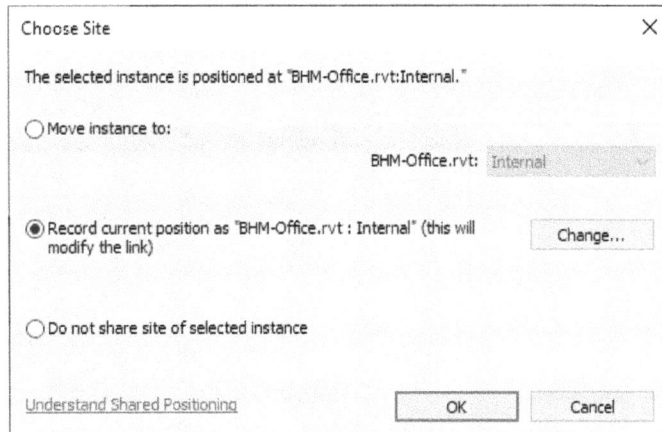

Figure 1–52

How To: Save the Recorded Locations' Positions to the Linked Model

When the coordinates from the host model have been published to linked models, they still need to be saved back to the linked file(s).

1. In the *Manage* tab>Manage Project panel, click ▣ (Manage Links).
2. In the Manage Links dialog box, select the *Revit* tab.

3. A check mark displays in the *Positions Not Saved* column, as shown in Figure 1–53, indicating that the published coordinates have not yet been saved to the linked model.

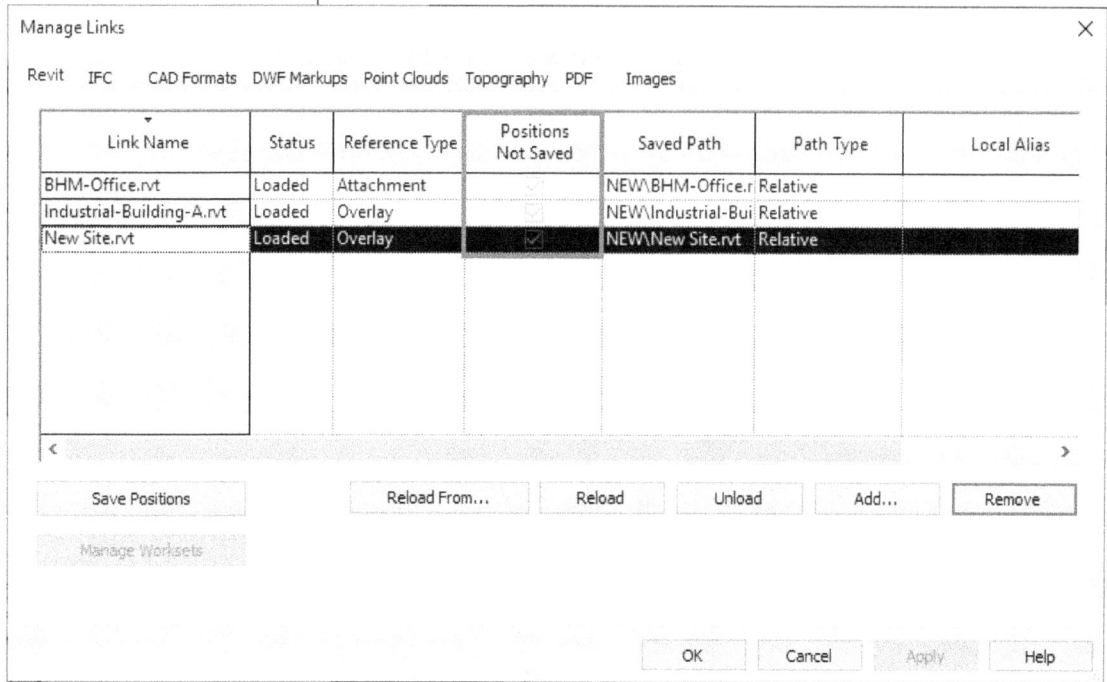

Manage Links   ✕

Revit   IFC   CAD Formats DWF Markups Point Clouds Topography PDF   Images

▾ Link Name	Status	Reference Type	Positions Not Saved	Saved Path	Path Type	Local Alias
BHM-Office.rvt	Loaded	Attachment		NEW\BHM-Office.r	Relative	
Industrial-Building-A.rvt	Loaded	Overlay		NEW\Industrial-Bui	Relative	
New Site.rvt	Loaded	Overlay	☑	NEW\New Site.rvt	Relative	

<   >

| Save Positions | | Reload From... | Reload | Unload | Add... | Remove |

Manage Worksets

OK   Cancel   Apply   Help

Figure 1–53

4. Select the name in the *Linked File* column and click **Save Positions**.

5. In the Location Position Changed dialog box, shown in Figure 1–54, select the method that you want to use.

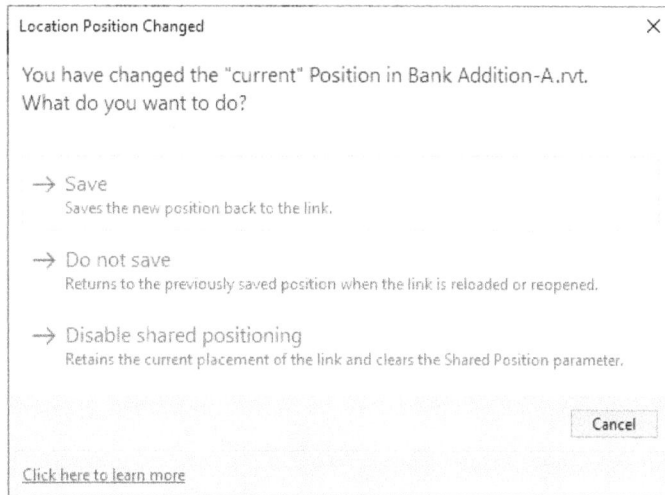

Figure 1–54

6. If you select **Save**, the *Positions Not Saved* option is cleared in the Manage Links dialog box.
7. Click **OK** to close the dialog box.

If you make a change to the location or save the project before managing the links, you are prompted to make a selection in the same dialog box.

Practice 1b

Working with Shared Coordinates

Practice Objectives

- Link a model to a site host project multiple times.
- Publish coordinates and share locations.
- Test different locations.

In this practice, you will link a project to a site multiple times, publish coordinates, and share locations. You will also test different locations using shared coordinates, as shown in Figure 1–55.

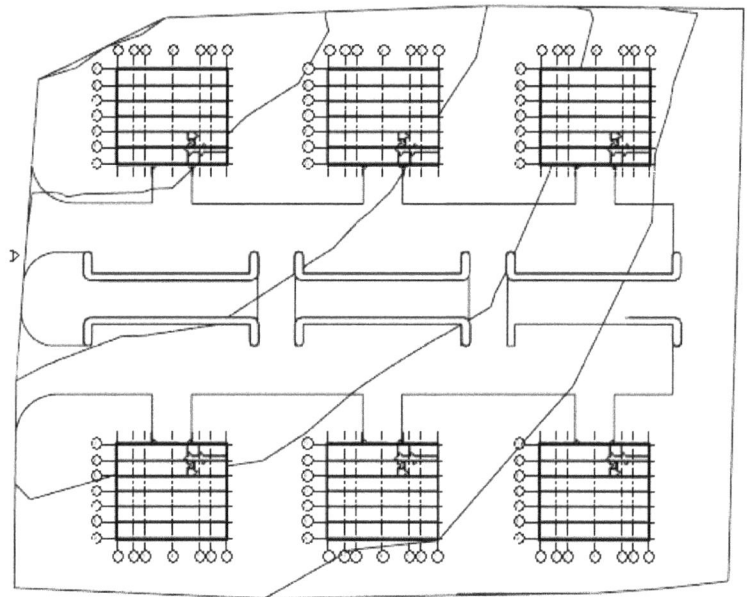

Figure 1–55

Task 1 - Link the architectural project to the site.

1. In the practice files folder, open **Industrial-Park-M.rvt**.

2. In the *Insert* tab>Link panel, click (Link Revit).

3. In the Import/Link RVT dialog box, select **Industrial-Building-A-M.rvt** and set the *Positioning* to **Auto - Internal Origin to Internal Origin**. Click **Open**.

4. Move the link so that the upper left corner meets the intersection of the two reference planes, as shown in Figure 1–56.

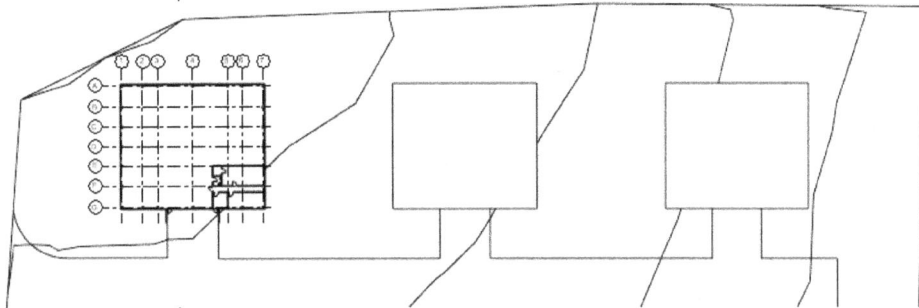

Figure 1–56

5. Select the link. In Properties, under the *Identity Data* section, type **Building A** for the *Name*, as shown in Figure 1–57. Do not modify the *Shared Site* parameter at this time.

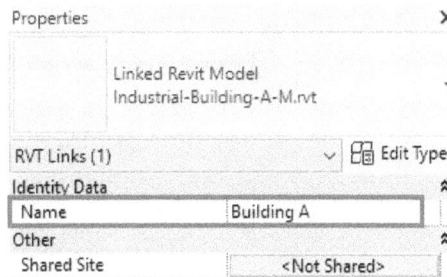

Figure 1–57

Task 2 - Publish coordinates and share locations.

1. In the *Manage* tab>Project Location panel, expand ⬈ (Coordinates) and select ⬈ (Publish Coordinates).

2. Select the link that you named **Building A**.

3. In the Location and Site dialog box, on the *Site* tab, click **Rename...** and rename the location to **Lot 1**, as shown in Figure 1–58. Click **OK** twice.

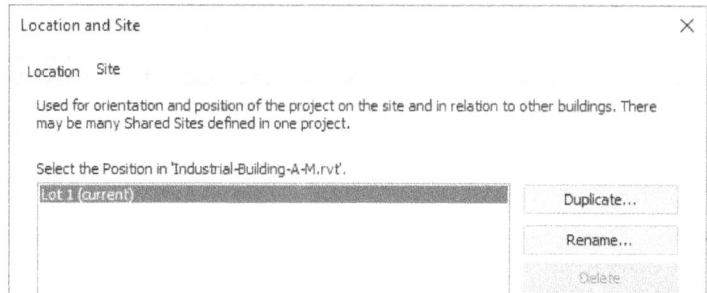

Figure 1–58

4. Save the file.

5. In the Location Position Changed dialog box, select **Save** (as shown in Figure 1–59) to save the position back to the linked architectural **Industrial-Building-A-M.rvt** file.

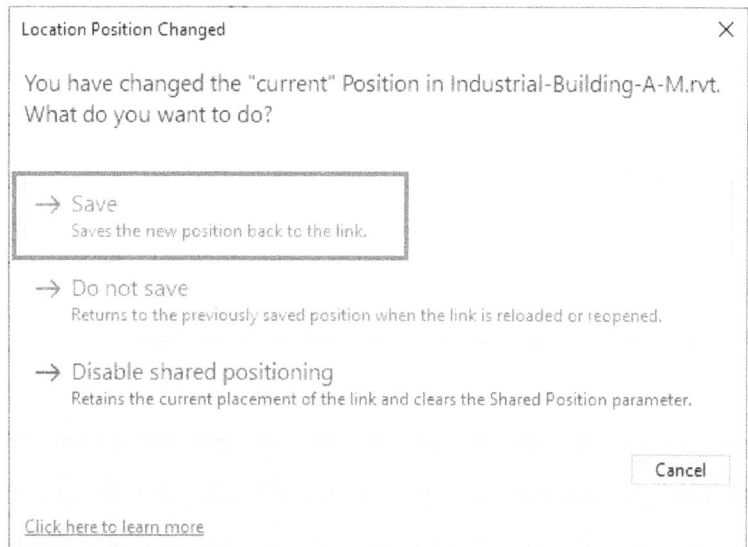

Figure 1–59

6. Close the project.

Task 3 - Acquire coordinates in the structural project from the architectural project.

---

1. Open **Industrial-Building-S-M.rvt** from the practice files folder.

2. In the view, select the linked file **Industrial-Building-A-M.rvt**. Note that in Properties, the *Shared Site* is set to **<Not Shared>**, as shown in Figure 1–60.

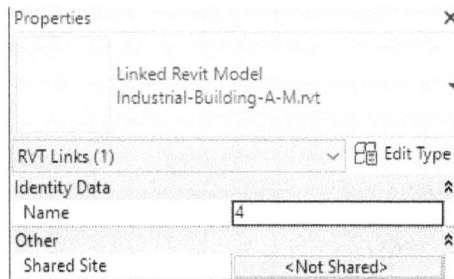

Figure 1–60

3. In the *Manage* tab>Project Location panel, expand

   ![Coordinates icon] (Coordinates) and select ![Acquire Coordinates icon] (Acquire Coordinates). Select the **Industrial-Building-A-M.rvt** link, as shown in Figure 1–61.

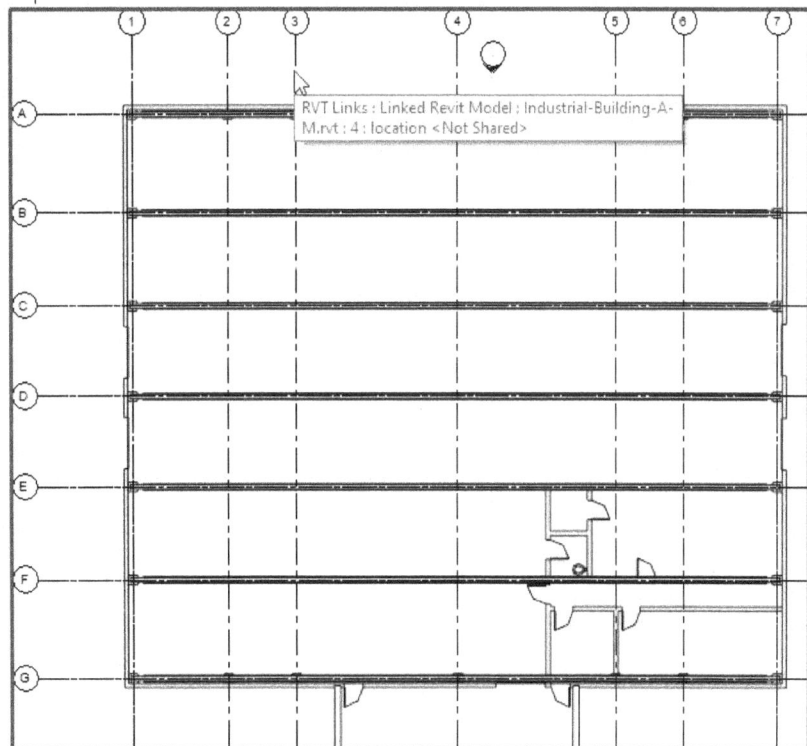

Figure 1–61

4. Click **Close** in the Acquire Coordinates Succeed dialog box.

5. Select the linked file and note that in Properties, the *Shared Site* shows **Lot 1**, as shown in Figure 1–62.

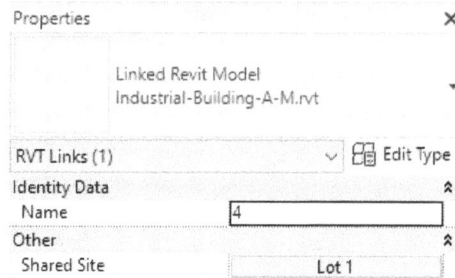

Figure 1–62

6. Save and close the project.

Task 4 - Set shared coordinates.

---

1. Open **Industrial-Park-M.rvt** from the practice files folder.

2. In the *Insert* tab>Link panel, click ⬛ (Link Revit).

3. In the Import/Link RVT dialog box, select **Industrial-Building-S-M.rvt** and set the *Positioning* to **Auto - By Shared Coordinates**. Click **Open**.

4. Click **Close** in the Nested Links Invisible dialog box.

5. The structural link goes on top of the **Industrial-Building-A-M.rvt** link you moved earlier in Task 1.

Use ▽ (Filter) to filter out the building pad or any other elements that might get selected.

6. Select both linked files and copy them to the other two top lots so that they are on top of the building pads, as shown in Figure 1–63.

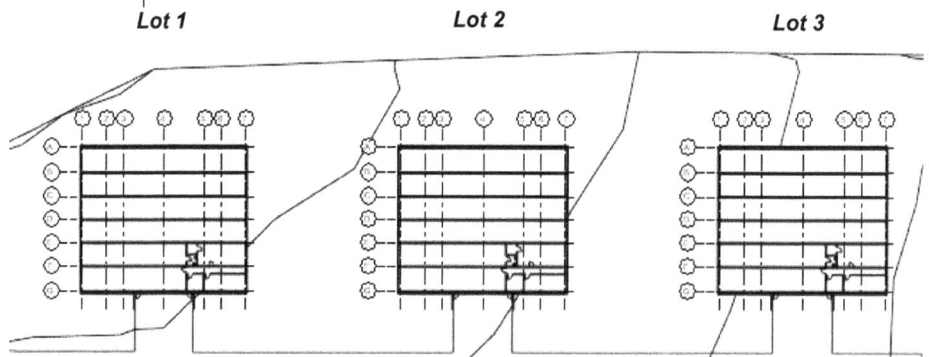

Figure 1–63

7. Open the Visibility/Graphic Overrides dialog box.

8. In the *Revit Links* tab, uncheck **Industrial-Building-A-M.rvt**, as shown in Figure 1–64. Click **OK**.

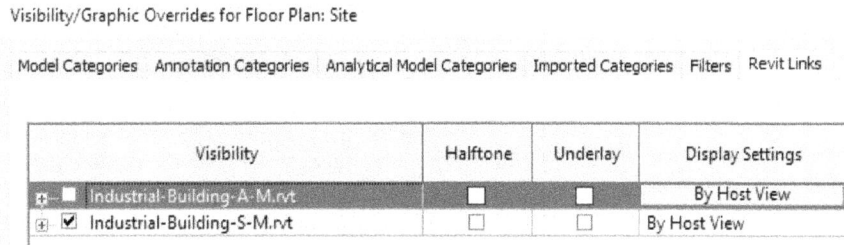

Visibility/Graphic Overrides for Floor Plan: Site

Model Categories Annotation Categories Analytical Model Categories Imported Categories Filters Revit Links

Visibility	Halftone	Underlay	Display Settings
Industrial-Building-A-M.rvt	☐	☐	By Host View
✔ Industrial-Building-S-M.rvt	☐	☐	By Host View

Figure 1–64

9. Select the first structural link and, in Properties, under the *Identity Data* section, type **Structure A** for the *Name* (as shown in Figure 1–65). Click in an empty area in the view to clear the selection.

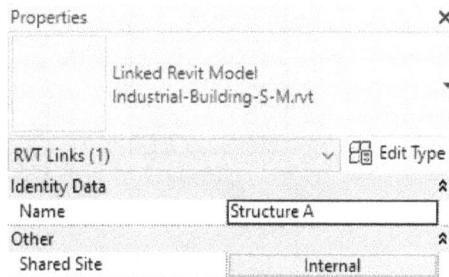

Properties   ✕

Linked Revit Model
Industrial-Building-S-M.rvt   ▾

RVT Links (1)   ∨   Edit Type

Identity Data		≫
Name	Structure A	
Other		≫
Shared Site	Internal	

Figure 1–65

10. Repeat Step 9 for the other two links, naming them **Structure B** and **Structure C**.

11. Open the Visibility/Graphic Overrides dialog box.

12. In the *Revit Links* tab, check **Industrial-Building-A-M.rvt** and uncheck **Industrial-Building-S-M.rvt**, as shown in Figure 1–66. Click **OK**.

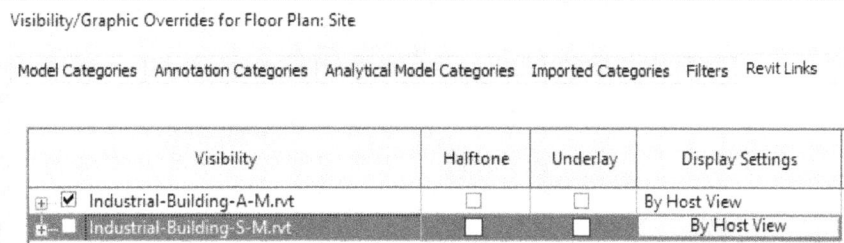

Visibility/Graphic Overrides for Floor Plan: Site

Model Categories Annotation Categories Analytical Model Categories Imported Categories Filters Revit Links

Visibility	Halftone	Underlay	Display Settings
✔ Industrial-Building-A-M.rvt	☐	☐	By Host View
Industrial-Building-S-M.rvt	☐	☐	By Host View

Figure 1–66

13. Select the copied architectural link and, in Properties, under the *Identity Data* section, type **Building B** for the *Name* (as shown in Figure 1–67).

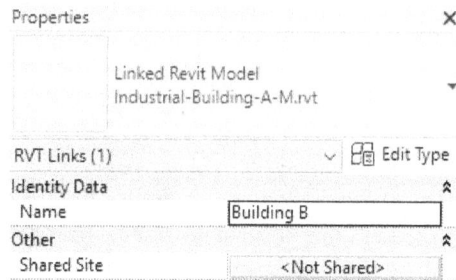

Figure 1–67

14. Click in an empty area in the view to clear the selection, then select the next architectural link (as shown in Figure 1–68) and name it **Building C**.

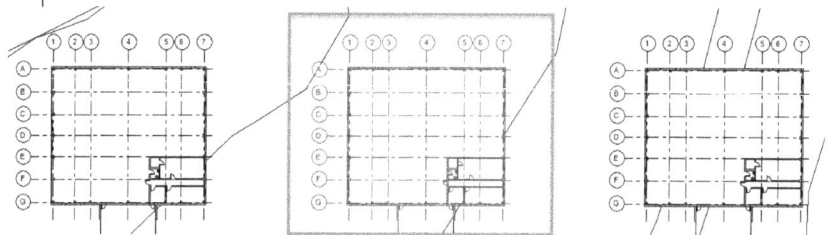

Figure 1–68

15. In the view, select the **Building B** link in the second lot, and in Properties, click **<Not Shared>** next to *Shared Site*.

16. In the Choose Site dialog box, click **Change...**, as shown in Figure 1–69.

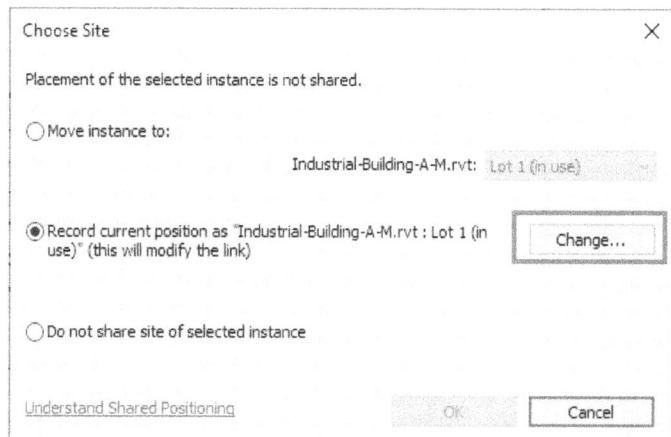

Figure 1–69

17. In the Location and Site dialog box, click **Duplicate...**. In the Name dialog box, type **Lot 2** and click **OK**.

18. Click **OK** twice to return to the view.

19. Select the **Building C** link and repeat Steps 14 to 17, naming the duplicated position **Lot 3**, as shown in Figure 1–70.

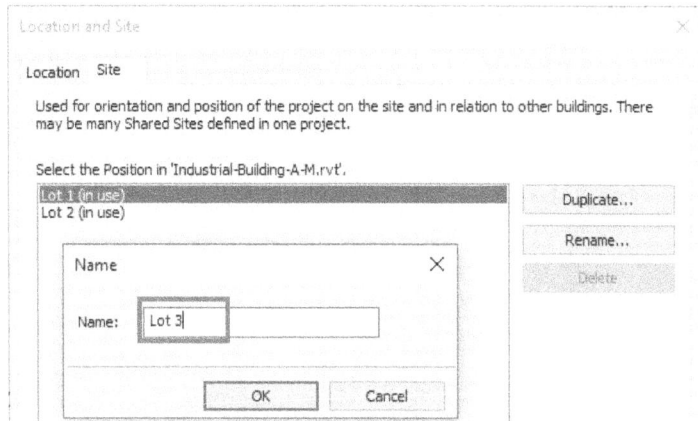

Figure 1–70

20. Open the Visibility/Graphic Overrides dialog box.

21. In the *Revit Links* tab, check **Industrial-Building-S-M.rvt** and uncheck **Industrial-Building-A-M.rvt**, as shown in Figure 1–71. Click **OK**.

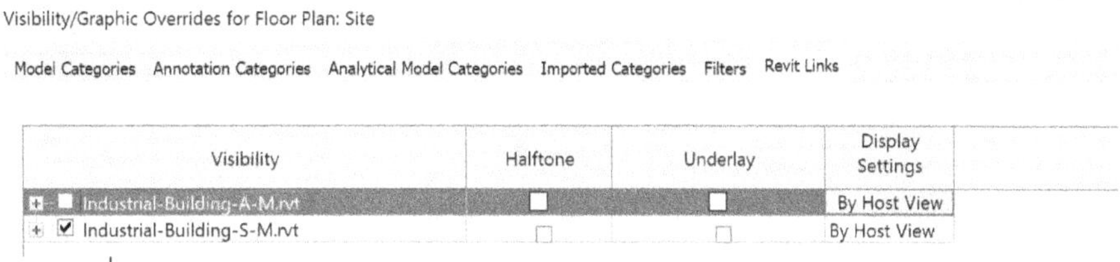

Figure 1–71

22. In the view, select the **Structure A** link, and in Properties, click on **<Internal>** next to *Shared Site*.

23. In the Choose Site dialog box, click **Change...**.

24. In the Location and Site dialog box, click **Rename...** and rename the Internal position to **Lot 1**, as shown in Figure 1–72. Click **OK** three times to return to the view.

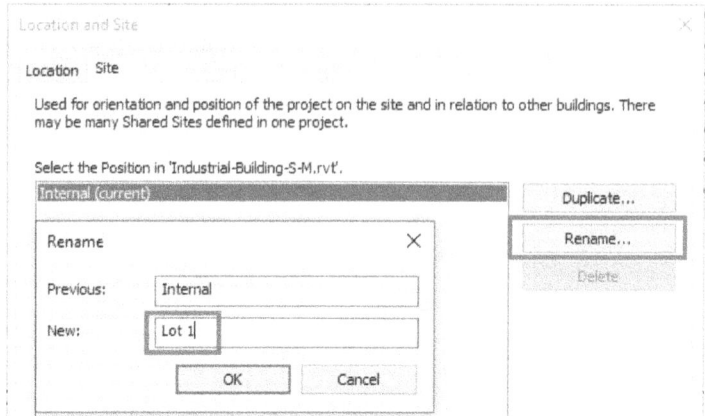

Figure 1–72

25. Select the **Structure B** link and repeat Steps 22 and 23, but this time, click **Duplicate...** and name the position **Lot 2**. Repeat the same steps for the **Structure C** link, duplicate the position, and name it **Lot 3**.

26. Open the Visibility/Graphic Overrides dialog box. In the *Revit Links* tab, check both linked files and click **OK**.

27. In the *Insert* tab>Link panel, select 🖼 (Manage Links).

28. In the *Revit* tab, select **Industrial-Building-A-M.rvt** and click **Save Positions**, as shown in Figure 1–73.

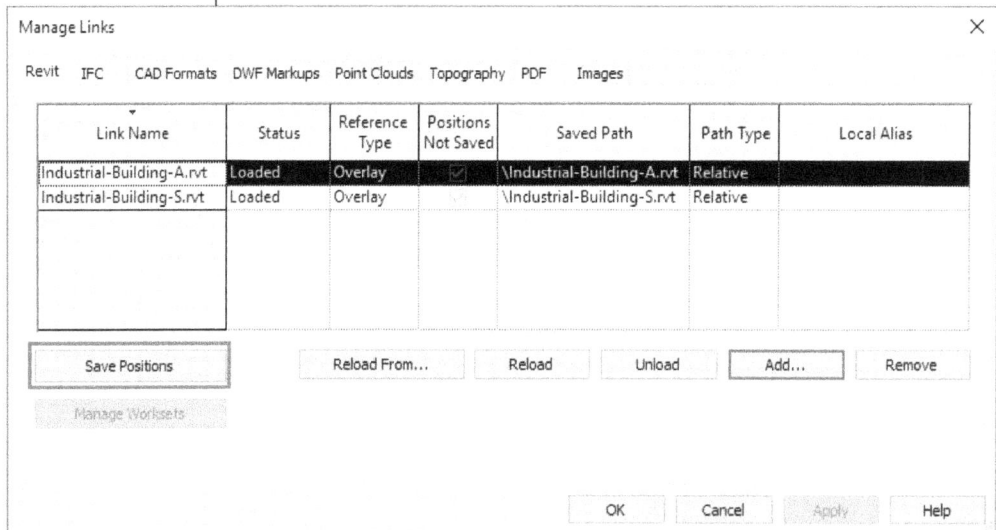

Figure 1–73

29. In the Location Position Changed dialog box, select **Save**, which saves the new position back to the linked architectural file.

30. Select **Industrial-Building-S-M.rvt** and click **Save Positions**. Select **Save** in the Location Position Changed dialog box.

31. Set the *Reference Type* to **Attachment** for both links to display any nested links, as shown in Figure 1–74. Note that the *Positions Not Saved* checkboxes for both linked files are unchecked, meaning the positions have been saved.

Manage Links   ✕

Revit   IFC   CAD Formats   DWF Markups   Point Clouds   Topography   PDF   Images

Link Name	Status	Reference Type	Positions Not Saved	Saved Path	Path Type	Local Alias
Industrial-Building-A-M.rvt	Loaded	Attachment		Industrial-Building-A-M.rvt	Relative	
Industrial-Building-S-M.rvt	Loaded	Attachment		Industrial-Building-S-M.rvt	Relative	

Figure 1–74

32. Click **OK**.

33. Save the project.

Task 5 - Move instances to new sites.

In this task, you will see how the named positions that you created in the previous tasks will remember their locations even if the copied linked models are deleted from the project.

1. In the view, delete both links on Lot 2 and Lot 3, as shown in Figure 1–75.

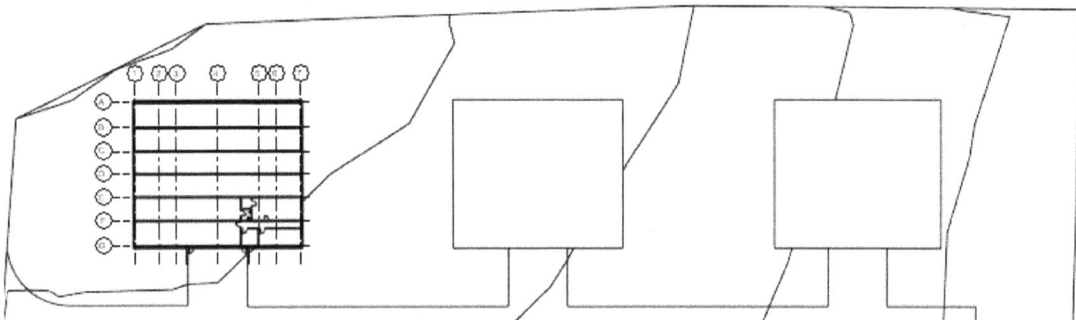

Figure 1–75

2. From Lot 1, select the **Industrial-Building-A-M.rvt** link and copy it two times over to the right side of the site. Do the same with the **Industrial-Building-S-M.rvt** link. It should look similar to what you see in Figure 1–76.

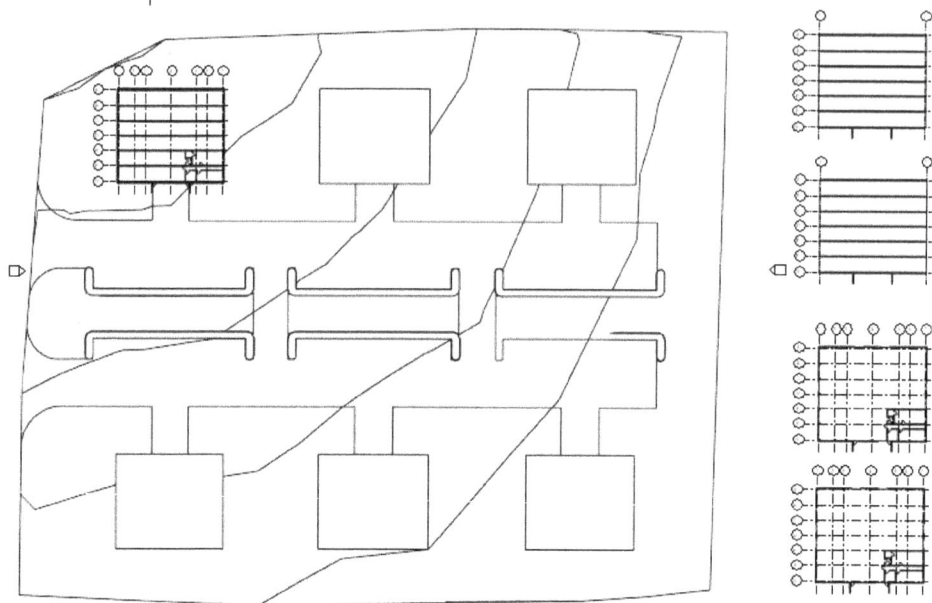

Figure 1–76

3. Select one of the copied **Industrial-Building-A-M.rvt** links off to the right side of the site.

   • If needed, you can rename the new copied instances in Properties.

4. In Properties, click **<Not Shared>** next to *Shared Site*.

5. In the Choose Site dialog box, select **Move instance to:** and set it to **Lot 2**, as shown in Figure 1–77. Click **OK**.

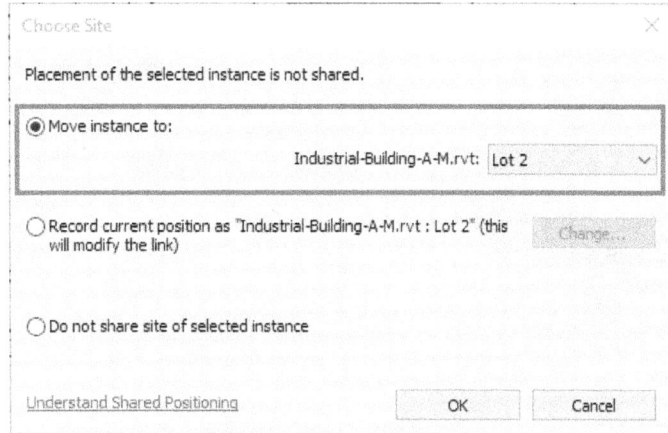

Figure 1–77

• The link will move into the Lot 2 position, as shown in Figure 1–78.

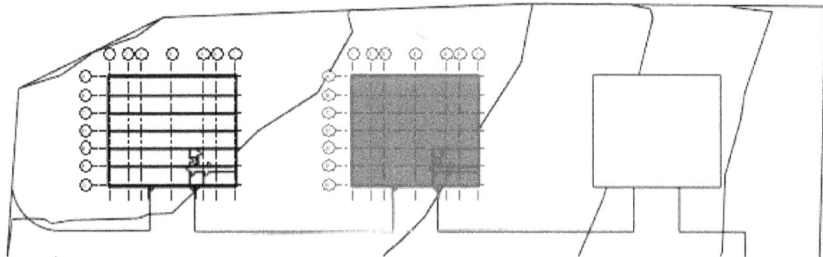

Figure 1–78

6. Repeat Steps 3 to 5 for the other links to move them into the correct positions.

7. Save and close the project.

1.5 Exporting to CAD Format

Exporting Revit projects to various CAD file formats is a common need in collaboration with consultants and engineers. Using this process, you can export individual views or sets of views to .DWG or .DXF, as shown in Figure 1–79, and keep the shared coordinate intact. You can also create and save sets of views to use again if needed.

Scroll down the Export list to see additional options.

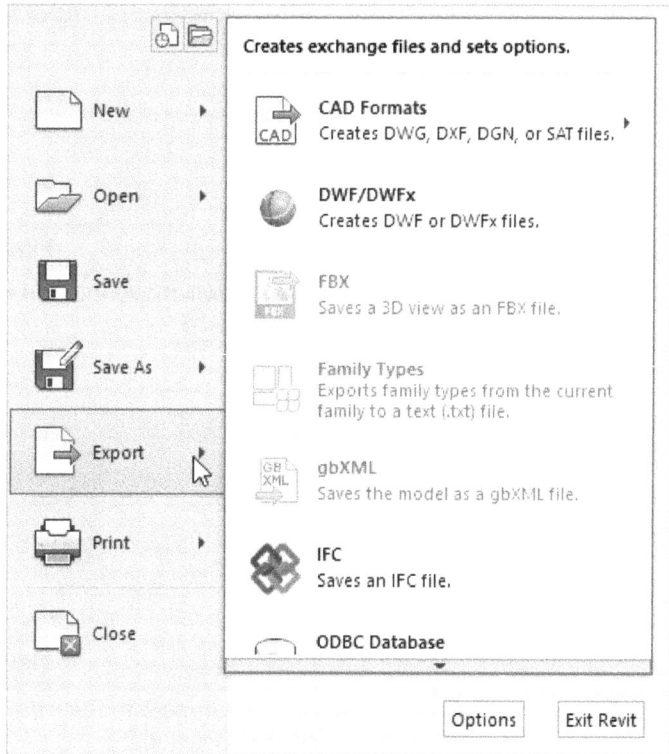

Figure 1–79

- To improve performance and file size of the exported file, you will want to use Visibility/Graphic Overrides to turn off objects that are not being seen in the view you are exporting.

- Use a section box or crop region to minimize elements outside the region.

- Reduce the amount of detail by setting the view's detail level to **Coarse** or **Medium**.

- In order for shared coordinates to work properly, only Revit views can be exported to .DWG.

How To: Create an Export Setup

1. In the DWG or DXF Export dialog box, next to the *Select Export Setup* list, click ⬚ (Modify Export Setup), or in the *File* tab, expand 🔲 (Export), scroll down to 🔧 (Options), expand it, and select 📄 (Export Setups DWG/DXF) or 📄 (Export Setups DGN).

2. The Modify DWG/DXF Export Setup or Modify DGN Export Setup dialog box contains all of the elements and types you can export. You can select an existing layer standard provided with the program (as shown in Figure 1–80) or create a new one.

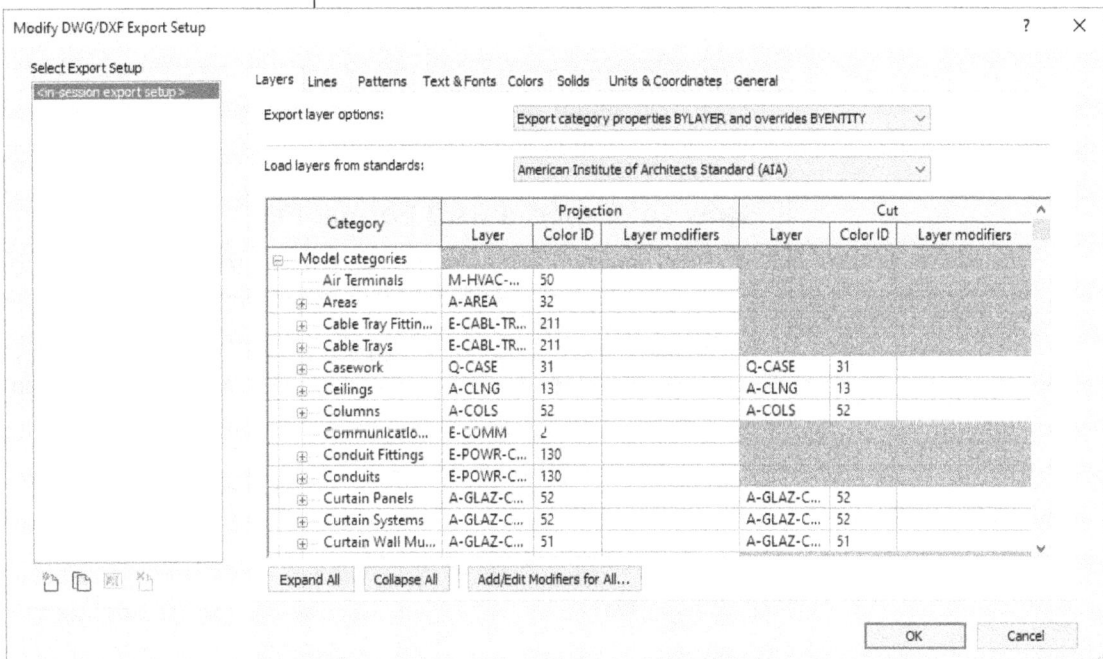

Figure 1–80

3. Select each of the tabs and apply the appropriate information.

- In the *Layers* tab, map the categories in Revit to the layers (or levels).

- In the *Lines*, *Patterns*, and *Text & Fonts* tabs, map the styles required.

- In the *Colors* tab, select to export either Index colors (255 colors) or True color (RGB values).

- In the *Solids* tab (3D views only), select to export to either Polymesh or ACIS solids.
- In the *Units & Coordinates* tab, specify what unit type one DWG unit is and the basis for the coordinate system. In order for the exported Revit file to be in the correct location when XREFed into AutoCAD, you will need to make sure the unit is correct.
  - **Shared Coordinates:** Use this method if you want to maintain the shared coordinates of the Revit host model.
  - **Internal Origin:** Use this method if you have not used shared coordinates in the Revit host model.
- In the *General* tab, you can set up how the rooms and room boundaries are exported; what to do with any non-plottable layers; how scope boxes, reference planes, coincident lines, and unreferenced view tags are handled; how views on sheets and links are treated; and which version of the DWG file format to use.
- Export setups can be created in a template file or shared between open projects using Transfer Project Standards.

How To: Export a CAD Format File

1. If you are exporting only one view, open the view you want to export. If you are exporting the model, open a 3D view.

2. In the *File* tab, expand 🗗 (Export), click 🗗 (CAD Formats), and select the type of format you want to export, as shown in Figure 1–81.

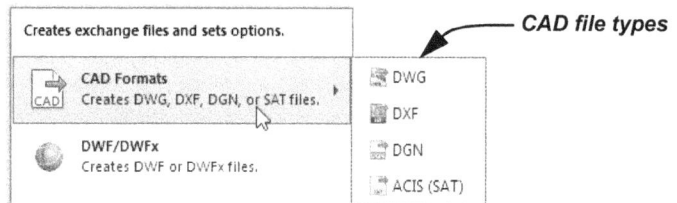

Figure 1–81

- The examples in this section show the process for .DWG files. It is the same for other types of files.

3. The DWG Export dialog box displays, as shown in Figure 1–82.

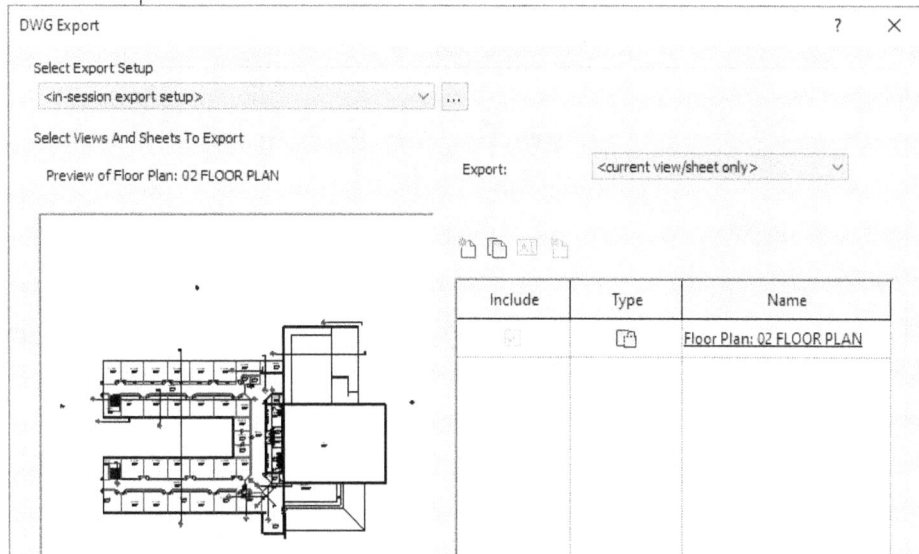

Figure 1–82

4. If you have an existing export setup, you can select it from the drop-down list (as shown in Figure 1–83) or click

   [...] (Modify Export Setup) to create a new one.

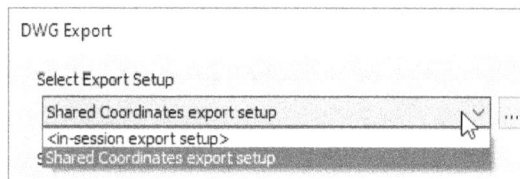

Figure 1–83

5. Select the view(s) you want to export from the Export drop-down list, as shown in Figure 1–84.

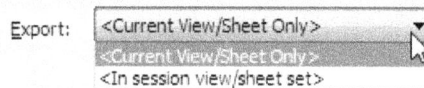

Figure 1–84

- To export only the active view, select **<Current View/ Sheet Only>**.
- To export any views or sheets that are open in the session of Revit, select **<In session view/sheet set>**.

6. When everything is set up correctly, click **Next...**.

7. In the Export CAD Formats - Save to Target Folder dialog box, select the folder location and name. If you are exporting to .DWG or .DXF, select the version in the Files of type drop-down list.

8. Click **OK**.

How To: Create a New Set of Views/Sheets to Export

1. Start the appropriate Export CAD Formats command.

2. In the Export CAD Formats dialog box, click (New Set).

3. In the New Set dialog box, type a name and click **OK**.

4. The tab displays with the new set active and additional information, as shown in Figure 1–85.

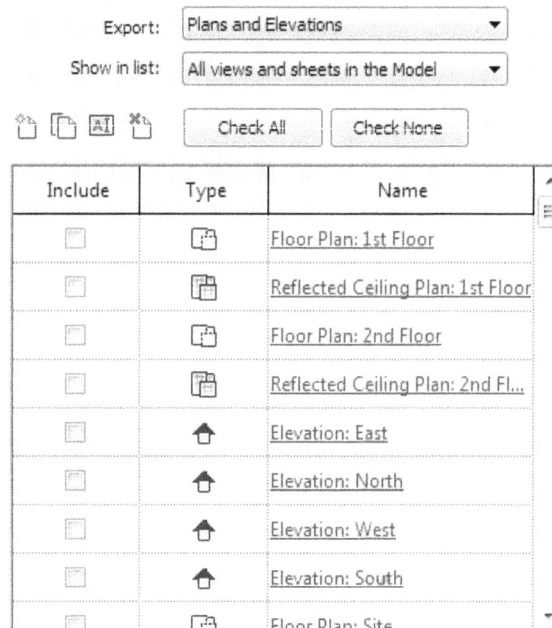

Include	Type	Name
		Floor Plan: 1st Floor
		Reflected Ceiling Plan: 1st Floor
		Floor Plan: 2nd Floor
		Reflected Ceiling Plan: 2nd Fl...
		Elevation: East
		Elevation: North
		Elevation: West
		Elevation: South
		Floor Plan: Site

Export: Plans and Elevations
Show in list: All views and sheets in the Model
Check All   Check None

Figure 1–85

5. Use *Show in List* to limit the number of items that display in the table.

6. Select the views and/or sheets that you want to export from the project.

   • Use **Check all** or **Check none** to aid in selection.

7. When you finish with the set, continue the export process.

Chapter Review Questions

1. The project base point defines the origin of the project coordinate system and impacts absolute elevations.

    a. True

    b. False

2. If you want a linked Revit model's internal origin to link in at your Revit model's internal origin, what link positioning method would you use?

    a. Manual - Internal Origin

    b. Auto - Project Base Point to Project Base Point

    c. Auto - By Shared Coordinates

    d. Auto - Internal Origin to Internal Origin

3. When you have a site plan linked to a host building project and want to adopt the link's shared coordinates, which of the following should you do?

    a. Relocate the project to the correct position.

    b. Acquire the coordinates from the site plan.

    c. Publish the coordinates to the site plan.

    d. Use Specify Coordinates at Point.

4. If you have acquired coordinates from a linked file, what do you need to do to share the coordinates with other linked files and models?

    a. Have the author of each file or model acquire their own coordinates.

    b. Publish the coordinates to the site plan.

    c. Publish the coordinates to the linked files and models.

5. You can publish coordinates to linked models through Instance Properties.

    a. True

    b. False

Command Summary

Button	Command	Location
	Acquire Coordinates	• **Ribbon:** *Manage* tab>Project Location panel>Coordinates drop-down list
	Import CAD	• **Ribbon:** *Insert* tab>Import panel
	Link CAD	• **Ribbon:** *Insert* tab>Link panel
	Link Revit	• **Ribbon:** *Insert* tab>Link panel
	Link Topography	• **Ribbon:** *Insert* tab>Link panel
	Location	• **Ribbon:** *Manage* tab>Project Location panel
	Manage Links	• **Ribbon:** *Manage* tab>Manage Projects panel • **Ribbon:** *Insert* tab>Link
	Pin	• **Ribbon:** *Modify* tab>Modify panel
	Publish Coordinates	• **Ribbon:** *Manage* tab>Project Location panel>Coordinates drop-down list
	Relocate Project	• **Ribbon:** *Manage* tab>Project Location panel>Position drop-down list
	Report Shared Coordinates	• **Ribbon:** *Manage* tab>Project Location panel>Coordinates drop-down list
	Reset Coordinates	• **Ribbon:** *Manage* tab>Project Location panel>Coordinates drop-down list
	Specify Coordinates at Point	• **Ribbon:** *Manage* tab>Project Location panel>Coordinates drop-down list

Site Design

In Revit®, you can create topographical surfaces (toposurfaces) and make basic modifications to them. These toposurfaces can be sketched directly in the project or linked into the project using a .DWG, .TXT or .CSV file provided by the surveyor or civil engineer. Once you have a toposurface in place, you can add property lines, cut out space for a building pad, create a new surface, or add/delete and modify elevations. Toposurfaces can support components such as parking spaces and trees.

Learning Objectives in This Chapter

- Create toposurfaces and add property lines and building pads.
- Create subregions of a toposurface.
- Split and merge the surfaces of a toposurface.
- Grade toposurfaces.
- Annotate toposurfaces.
- Add site and parking components to toposurfaces.

2.1 Creating Topographical Surfaces

You can create topographical surfaces (toposurfaces) from an imported CAD, .TXT, or .CVS file developed by a surveyor or civil engineer, as shown in Figure 2–1. Once the toposurface is created, you can edit individual points and modify the site settings.

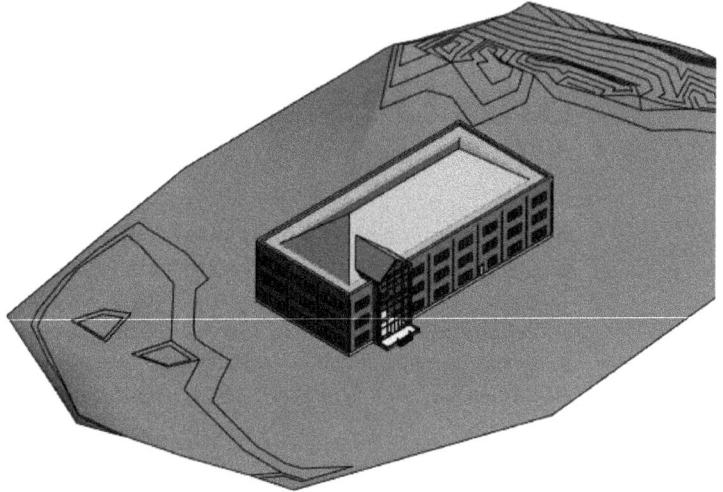

Figure 2–1

- Note that you can link an Autodesk Civil 3D topography file, but doing so requires you to have access to BIM 360.

How To: Create a Toposurface by Specifying Points

1. Open a site or 3D view.
2. In the *Massing & Site* tab>Model Site panel, click

   (Toposurface).
3. In the *Modify | Edit Surface* tab>Tools panel, click (Place Point).
4. In the Options Bar, set the *Elevation* for the point, as shown in Figure 2–2. By default, you are only able to select **Absolute Elevation**. After you create a surface of three points, you can also select **Relative to Surface**.

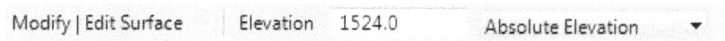

Figure 2–2

5. Click in the drawing area to place the point.

6. Continue placing points. You can vary the elevation as needed. After you have placed three points, a boundary is displayed, connecting them. When you add a point at a different elevation, you see the contour lines forming, as shown in Figure 2–3.

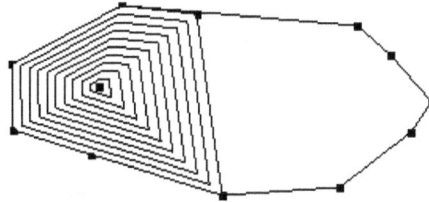

Figure 2–3

7. In the Surface panel, click ✔ (Finish Surface) when you have finished selecting points.

• Points can be added in plan and 3D views and site plans.

• To create a neat outer boundary for a toposurface, use model lines so you can see this boundary in a 3D view. You can draw reference planes and then select points at the intersections of the planes. Reference planes will not appear in a 3D view.

How To: Create a Toposurface Using an Imported File

1. In a site or 3D view, import a CAD file (.DWG, .DXF, or .DGN) that holds the site information.
   • When importing, do not use the **Current view only** option as you need the 3D information stored in the CAD file.
2. In the *Massing & Site* tab>Model Site panel, click
   (Toposurface).
3. In the *Modify | Edit Surface* tab>Tools panel, expand
   (Create from Import) and click (Select Import Instance).
4. Select the imported file by clicking on the edge of the file.

5. In the Add Points from Selected Layers dialog box, select the layers or levels that hold the points (the layer names vary according to the original drawing file standard), as shown in Figure 2–4.

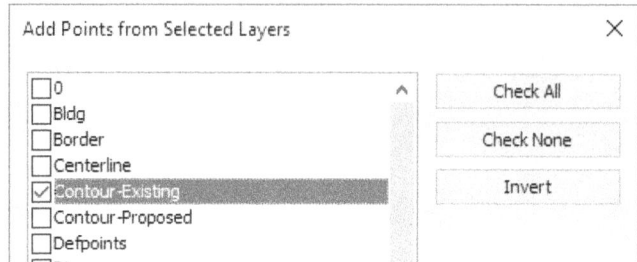

Figure 2–4

6. Click **OK**. The new toposurface is created with points at the same elevations as the imported information.

7. Click �🗸 (Finish Surface) to end the command.
8. If the CAD file is not needed, it can be hidden in the view or unloaded in the Manage Links dialog box if the CAD file is linked into the model.

   • If the CAD file is going to be updated with information (such as the footprint of the building or roads and parking areas), it would be better to link the CAD file. This way, when the up-to-date information is provided, it is included in the project.

How To: Create a Toposurface from a Points File

1. Open a site or 3D view. In the *Massing & Site* tab>Model Site panel, click 🖾 (Toposurface).
2. In the *Modify | Edit Surface* tab>Tools panel, expand

   🖾 (Create from Import) and click 🖾 (Specify Points File).
3. In the Select File dialog box, select the .CSV or comma delimited text file (.TXT) that contains the list of points and click **Open**.
4. In the Format dialog box (shown in Figure 2–5), select the unit format and click **OK**. The options include **Centimeters, Feet, Inches, Meters**, and **Millimeters**.

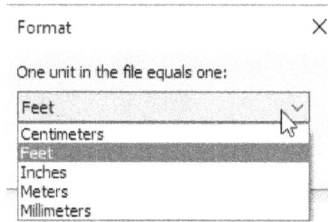

Figure 2–5

5. The points create a toposurface in the project. Add additional points as needed and click ✓ (Finish Surface).

•   Having many points on a surface slows down system performance. While still in the *Modify | Edit Surface* tab> Tools panel, click ⌂ (Simplify Surface) to reduce the number of points. Set the required accuracy, as shown in Figure 2–6, and click **OK**.

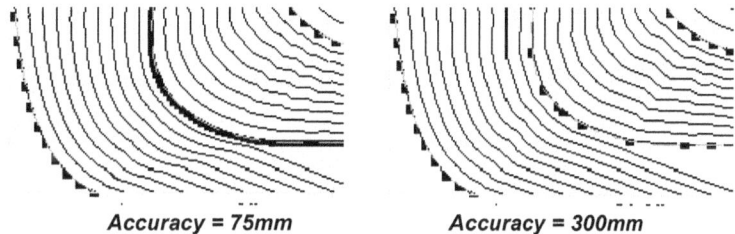

Accuracy = 75mm   *Accuracy = 300mm*

Figure 2–6

Editing Toposurfaces

You can make changes to a toposurface by adding points or editing existing point locations and elevations, as shown in Figure 2–7. You can also modify the properties of a toposurface, including material and phasing information.

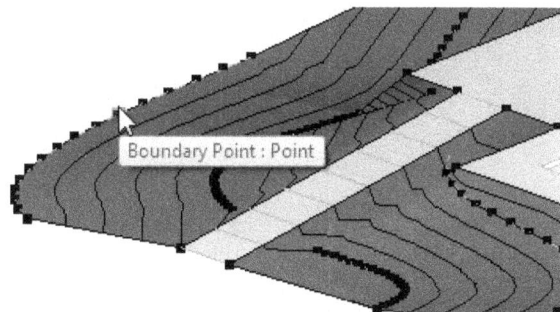

Figure 2–7

How To: Edit a Toposurface

1. Select the toposurface that you want to edit.
2. In the *Modify | Topography* tab>Surface panel, click ⬚ (Edit Surface).
3. In the *Modify | Edit Surface* tab>Tools panel, click ⬚ (Place Point) and add more points to the surface.
4. To edit existing points, select one or more points.
5. In the *Interior (or Boundary) Points* tab, you can use various modification tools. You can change the elevation of the points in the Options Bar, as shown in Figure 2–8.

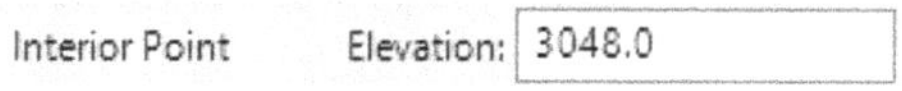

When adding points, it helps to be in a 3D shaded view so that you can see the effects of your new points.

Interior Point	Elevation:	3048.0

Figure 2–8

6. Select another point or click in an empty space to finish editing the points.
7. In the *Modify | Edit Surface* tab>Surface panel, click

   ⬚ (Finish Surface) to end the command.

Site Settings

In the *Massing & Site* tab>Model Site panel, click ⬚ in the panel title. The Site Settings dialog box opens, in which you can set the way contours are displayed in the plan and section views of a toposurface, as shown in Figure 2–9.

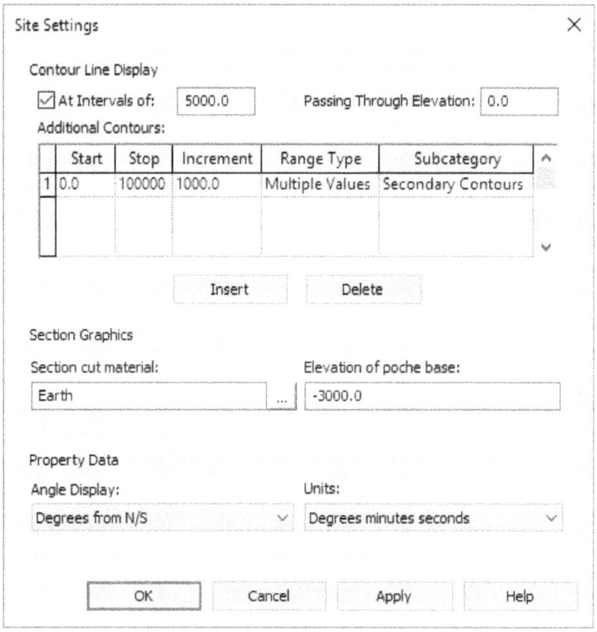

Figure 2–9

Site Setting Options

Contour Line Display

At Intervals of:	Set the distance for the primary contour lines. These display with a heavy line and are not necessarily the places at which you added the points.
Passing Through Elevation	The starting elevation for contour lines.

Additional Contours

Start/Stop	**Start** is the location for a single additional contour or the first of a series of contours. **Stop** is the end of a series of additional contour lines.
Increment	The distance between sub-contours when the *Range type* is set to **Multiple Values**. The style is set according to the Subcategory specification.
Range Type	When set to **Multiple Values**, you can specify the Start, Stop, and Increments. When set to **Single Value**, you can specify the location of the single contour in the **Start Value**. Stop and Increments are grayed out.
Subcategory	Select from a list of object styles that define how to display the additional contours. For example, **Secondary Contours** display with a thin line and **Primary Contours** with a wide line. You can create additional options in **Object Styles** under **Topography**.
Insert/Delete	Insert or delete additional contour descriptions.

Section Graphics

Section cut material	The default material is set to **Earth**. Click [...] (Browse) to open the Material Browser, in which you can select a different material. Additional site-related materials can be found in the *AEC Materials: Misc* area at the bottom of the Material Browser. The following shows a section cut using the **Earth** material.
Elevation of poche base	The height of the poche (or hatching) that displays below the bottom contour line in a section view. It is usually negative.

Property Data

Angle Display	Select the type of angles to display: **Degrees from N/S** or **Degrees**.
Units	Select the type of units to display: **Degrees Minutes Seconds** or **Decimal Degrees**.

Practice 2a

Create Topographical Surfaces

Practice Objectives

- Import a CAD file with contours.
- Set the project base point and the survey point.
- Create a toposurface from the imported file.
- (Optional) Create a toposurface using a points file.

In this practice, you will utilize the tools you learned in Chapter 1 by importing a CAD file that contains contour information, setting the project base point and survey point, creating a toposurface from the imported file, changing the site settings, and adding a section, as shown in Figure 2–10.

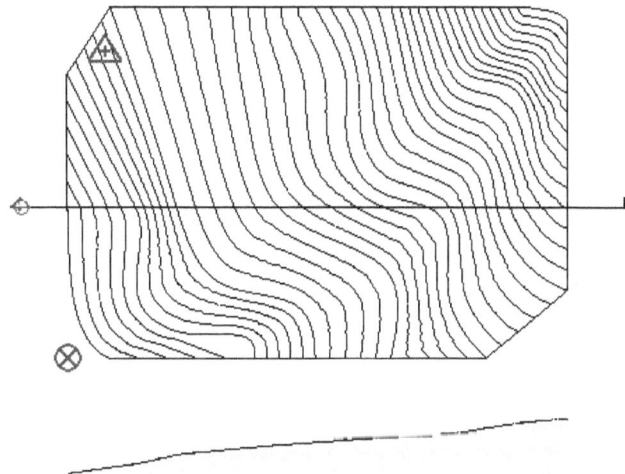

Figure 2–10

Task 1 - Import a CAD file.

1. Start a new project based on the Metric-Architectural Template.rte template (as shown in Figure 2–11) from the practice files *Template* folder.

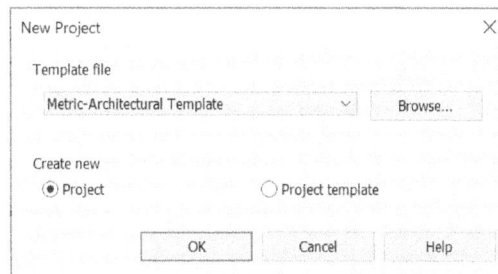

Figure 2–11

2. Open the **Floor Plans:Site** view.

3. Open the Visibility/Graphic Overrides dialog box (type **VV**) and turn on **Internal Origin** from the *Site* category on the *Model Categories* tab. This will show you the starting point.

4. Hide the elevation markers by selecting one, right-clicking, and selecting **Hide in View>Category**. Alternatively, select one elevation marker and type **VH** to hide in view by category.

5. In the *Insert* tab>Import panel, click 🗎 (Import CAD).

6. In the Import CAD Formats dialog box, navigate to the practice files *CAD* folder and select **Site-DWG-M.dwg**. Set the *Import units* to **Meter**, keep the other default options as is, and click **Open**.

7. Type **ZE** to zoom out to the extents of the file. The origin of the imported CAD file (0,0,0) is placed at the internal origin of the project, as shown in Figure 2–12.

This file was creating using the AutoCAD® software.

Figure 2–12

8. Save the project in the practice files folder as **New-Site-M.rvt**.

Task 2 - Set the project base point and the survey point.

1. In the site view, in the *Manage* tab>Project Location panel, expand **Coordinates** and select (Specify Coordinates at Point).

2. Click on the center of the three icons that are overlapping each other, as shown in Figure 2–13.

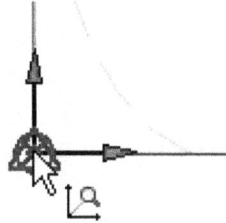

Figure 2–13

This is information you would receive from surveyors or civil engineers.

3. In the Specify Shared Coordinates dialog box, enter the following information, as shown in Figure 2–14:

   • *North/South*: **19202.4**
   • *East/West*: **22.9**
   • *Elevation*: **565708.8**

   (You will use a different method to change True North.)

Figure 2–14

4. Change the project base point's True North. In the view, select ⊗ (Project Base Point). Click the *Angle to True North* field, either in the view (as shown Figure 2–15) or in Properties (as shown in Figure 2–16), and enter **20**.

- Note that you can also set the *N/S*, *E/W*, and *Elev* in these two locations as well.

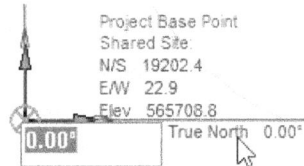

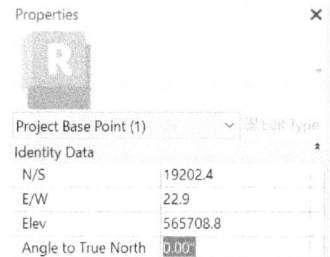

Figure 2–15   Figure 2–16

5. Type **ZA** to zoom all.

6. In the view, select ⬢ (Survey Point) and click 📎 (Change clip state of point) to unclip it.

- Note that properties will be grayed out when the survey point is clipped versus unclipped.

7. In Properties, set the information as follows (as shown in Figure 2–17):

- *N/S*: **107899.2**
- *E/W*: **68580.0**
- *Elev*: **568147.2**

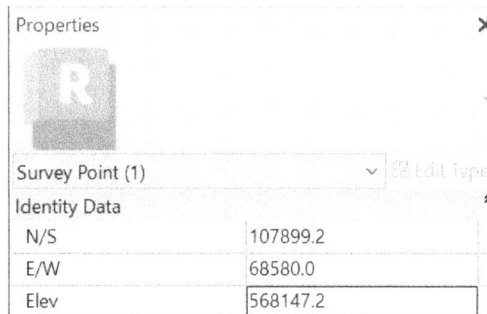

Figure 2–17

8. The survey point has moved to a new location. Click in an empty area away from the imported file in the view.

9. Select ⚠ (Survey Point) and click 🖉 (Change clip state of point) to re-clip the survey point in its new location.

10. Duplicate the **Floor Plans: Site** view and rename it **Site True North**.

11. In the **Floor Plans: Site True North** view, make sure nothing is selected. In Properties, change the *Orientation* to **True North** to rotate the site to true north (as shown in Figure 2–18).

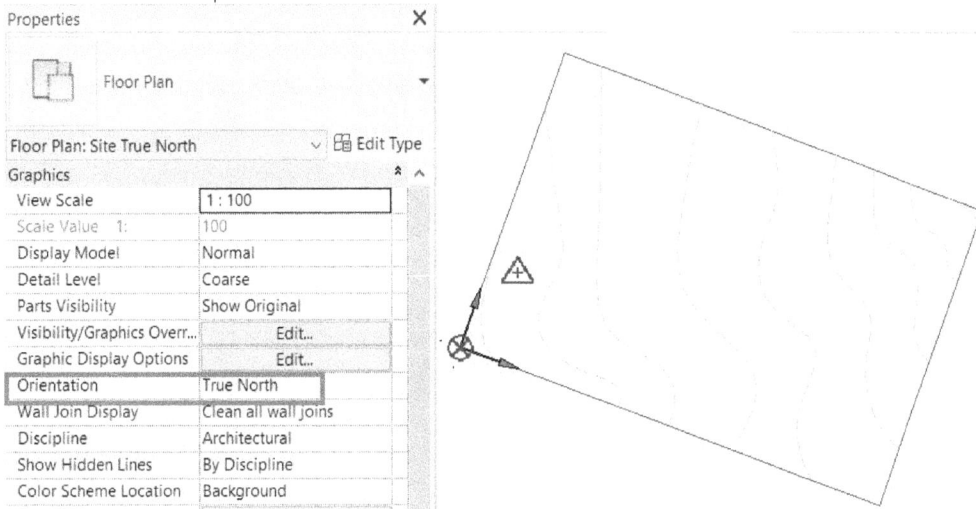

Figure 2–18

12. Save the project.

Task 3 - Create a toposurface from the imported file.

1. Open the **Floor Plans: Site** view.

2. In the *Massing & Site* tab>Model Site panel, click 🖾 (Toposurface).

3. In the *Modify | Edit Surface* tab>Tools panel, expand 🏠 (Create from Import) and click 🖾 (Select Import Instance).

4. Select the imported CAD file.

5. In the Add Points from Selected Layers dialog box, click **Check None**. Select **Contour-Existing** (as shown in Figure 2–19) and click **OK**.

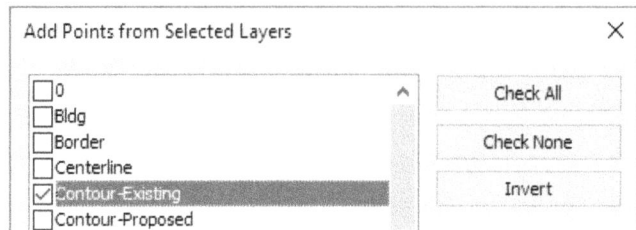

Figure 2–19

6. The new toposurface is created with points applied along the contour lines from the CAD file, as shown in Figure 2–20.

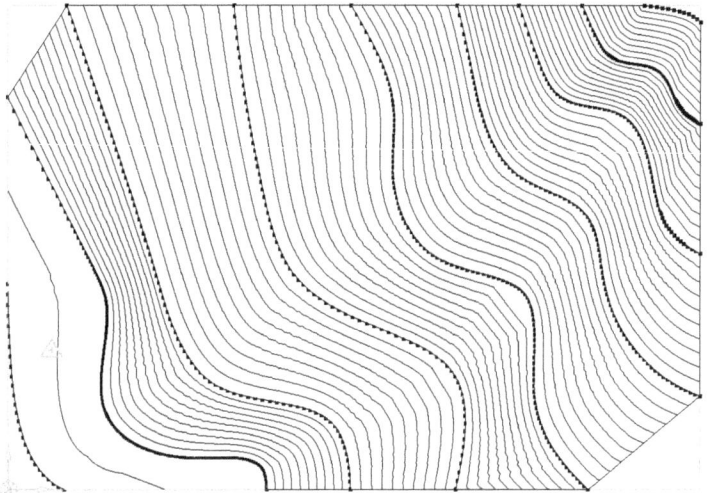

Figure 2–20

7. In the *Modify | Edit Surface* tab>Tools panel, click (Simplify Surface).

8. In the Simplify Surface dialog box, set the *Accuracy* to **300** (as shown in Figure 2–21) and click **OK**.

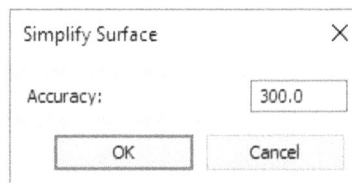

Figure 2–21

9. Fewer points are placed in the toposurface without compromising the actual contour location.

10. Click ✔ (Finish Surface).

11. Select the linked CAD file, click the pin at the center, and press <Delete>.

12. The contour lines should close together for better analysis and design purposes. This distance is specified in the Site Settings.In the *Massing & Site* tab>Model Site panel title, click ⬚ (Site Settings).

13. In the Site Settings dialog box, in the *Additional Contours* area, set the *Increment* to **2000**. Verify that the *Section cut material* is set to the **Earth** material and click **OK**. The distance between the contours changes, as shown in Figure 2–22.

Figure 2–22

14. Save the project.

Task 4 - Create a site section.

1. In the *View* tab>Create panel, click ⌖ (Section) and draw a horizontal section through the site.

2. In the Project Browser, in the *Section (Building Section)* node, rename the section as **Site Section**.

3. Open the section view and zoom in to see the material. The material displayed in the section is **Earth**, as shown in Figure 2–23, which was the default material in the Site Settings.

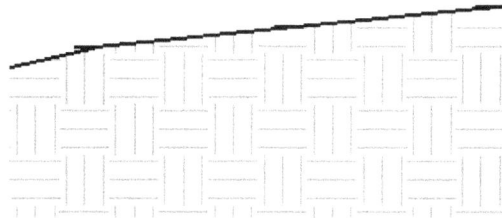

Figure 2–23

4. Open the **Elevations (Building Elevation): South** view.

5. Lengthen the levels to extend past the length of the site, as shown in Figure 2–24.

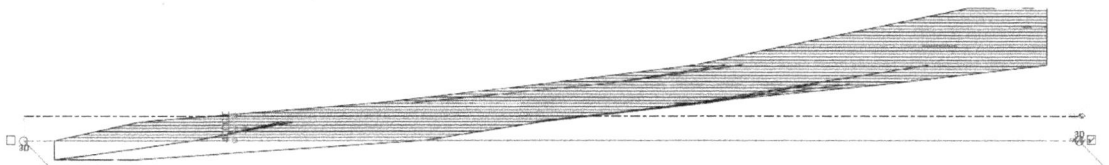

Figure 2–24

6. Click ☒ (Modify) and zoom in to the level heads to view what elevation they are at. By default, *Level 1* should be at **0**, as shown in Figure 2–25.

Level 2
4000

Level 1
0

Figure 2–25

7. Select one of the levels, then in Properties, click **Edit Type**. In the Type Properties dialog box, change the *Elevation Base* to **Survey Point** and click **OK**. The levels now reflect the elevation you specified when modifying the survey points earlier in the practice, as shown in Figure 2–26.

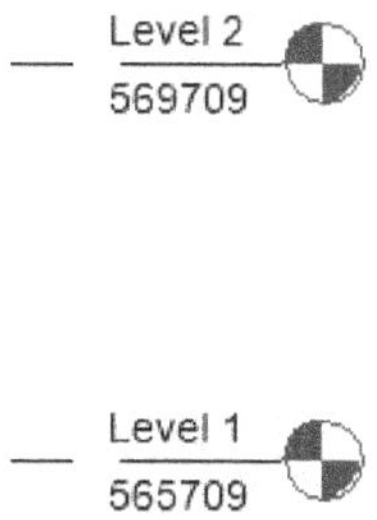

Figure 2–26

8. Save and close the project.

Task 5 - Create a toposurface using a points file.

1. Using Notepad or another text editor, in the practice files folder, open **Topography-Points-M.txt**. The list of points is partially shown in Figure 2–27 and includes three groups of numbers on each line. The format is **Northing (Y), Easting (X), Elevation**.

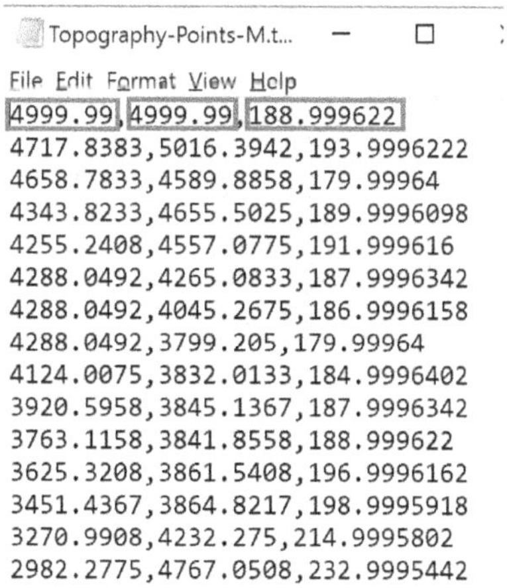

Topography-Points-M.t...

File Edit Format View Help

```
4999.99,4999.99,188.999622
4717.8383,5016.3942,193.9996222
4658.7833,4589.8858,179.99964
4343.8233,4655.5025,189.9996098
4255.2408,4557.0775,191.999616
4288.0492,4265.0833,187.9996342
4288.0492,4045.2675,186.9996158
4288.0492,3799.205,179.99964
4124.0075,3832.0133,184.9996402
3920.5958,3845.1367,187.9996342
3763.1158,3841.8558,188.999622
3625.3208,3861.5408,196.9996162
3451.4367,3864.8217,198.9995918
3270.9908,4232.275,214.9995802
2982.2775,4767.0508,232.9995442
```

Figure 2–27

2. Close the text file.

3. In the practice files folder, open **Topography-Points-M.rvt**.

4. Open the **Elevations (Building Elevation): South** view.

5. There are two levels. *Level 1* is set to **213360**, which works best with the information provided in the points file for the elevation, which ranges from 180 to 260 meters (180,000 to 260,000 mm).

6. Open the default 3D view.

7. In the *Massing & Site* tab>Model Site panel, click ▨ (Toposurface).

8. In the *Modify | Edit Surface* tab>Tools panel, expand 🏠 (Create from Import) and click 🏠 (Specify Points File).

9. In the Select File dialog box, navigate to the practice files folder, set the *Files of type* to **Comma delimited Text**, and select **Topography-Points-M.txt**. Click **Open**.

10. In the Format dialog box, select **Meters** and click **OK**.

11. Type **ZA** to zoom to the extents of the file.

12. Click ✓ (Finish Surface).

13. Zoom in on the toposurface and investigate it.

14. Orbit and pan around the site and modify the Site Settings, material, and visual style as needed to get a better understanding of the toposurface, as shown in Figure 2–28.

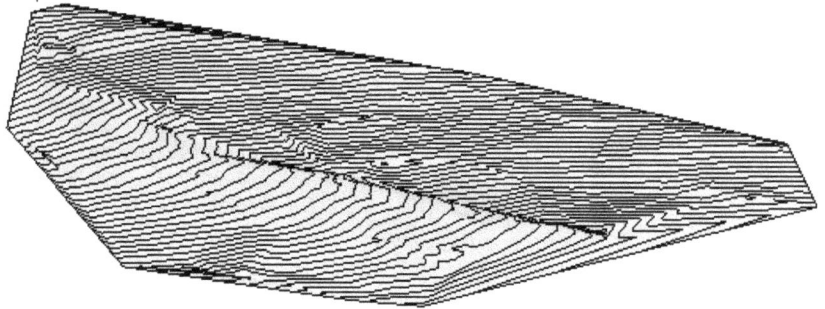

Figure 2–28

15. Save and close both of the projects.

2.2 Adding Property Lines and Building Pads

When you have placed the base toposurface, you can then add the property lines and building pad (the cutout for the building location), as shown in Figure 2–29.

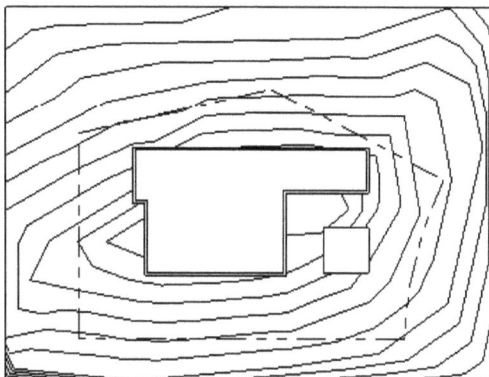

Figure 2–29

Creating Property Lines

Property lines can be created by sketching lines or can be table-based, where they are created by inputting information into a table of distances and bearings.

• By default, property lines are on display in the site view. To see them in other views, turn on Property Lines within the Visibility/Graphic Overrides dialog box under the *Site* category. (Property lines are not visible in any 3D view.)

• When drawing property lines, they should form a closed loop. If they do not form a closed loop, you will get a warning that you can ignore (as shown in Figure 2–30).

Warning

Property lines do not form a closed loop. Area will not be computed.

Figure 2–30

How To: Add a Property Line by Entering Distances and Bearings

1. In the *Massing & Site* tab>Modify Site panel, click

   ⌧ (Property Line).
2. In the Create Property Line dialog box, select **Create by entering distances and bearings**, as shown in Figure 2–31.

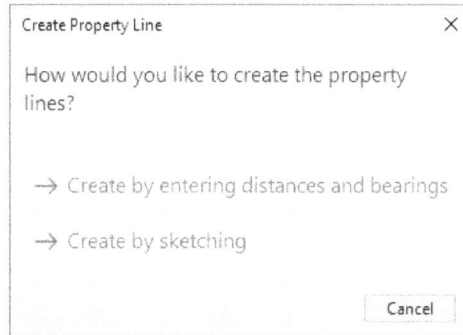

Create Property Line   ✕

How would you like to create the property lines?

→ Create by entering distances and bearings

→ Create by sketching

Cancel

Figure 2–31

3. In the Property Lines dialog box, fill out the appropriate information, as shown in Figure 2–32.

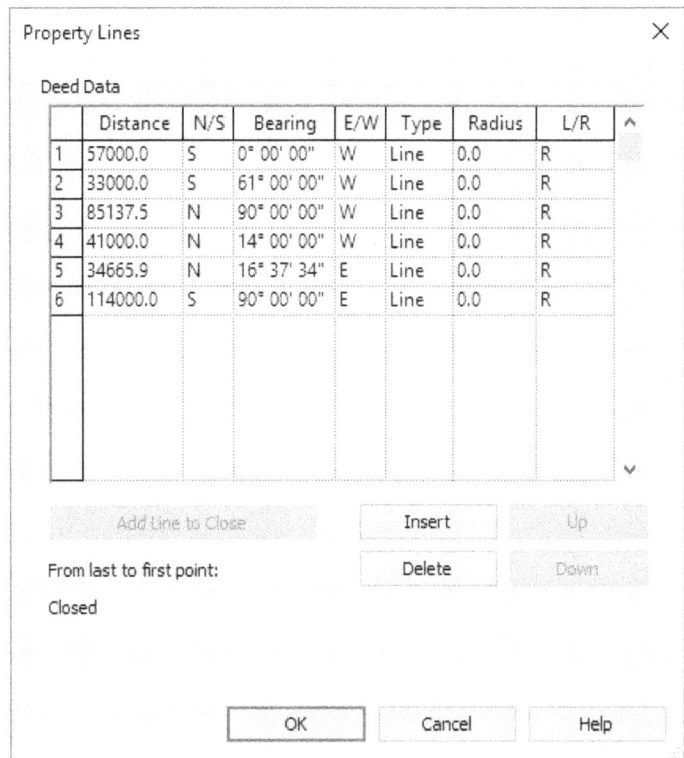

Property Lines   ✕

Deed Data

	Distance	N/S	Bearing	E/W	Type	Radius	L/R	^
1	57000.0	S	0° 00' 00"	W	Line	0.0	R	
2	33000.0	S	61° 00' 00"	W	Line	0.0	R	
3	85137.5	N	90° 00' 00"	W	Line	0.0	R	
4	41000.0	N	14° 00' 00"	W	Line	0.0	R	
5	34665.9	N	16° 37' 34"	E	Line	0.0	R	
6	114000.0	S	90° 00' 00"	E	Line	0.0	R	

Add Line to Close   Insert   Up

From last to first point: Delete   Down

Closed

OK   Cancel   Help

Figure 2–32

4. Click **Add Line to Close** to add a closing line.
5. Click **OK**.
6. In the view, click to place the property lines.

- When typing the bearings, you do not need to insert the symbols after the numbers, just separate them with a space. For example, 54 23 47 displays as 54° 23' 47".

- To edit table-based property lines, select on a line and in the *Modify | Property Lines* tab>Property Lines panel, select

  (Edit Table) to open the Property Lines dialog box.

How To: Add a Property Line by Sketching

1. In the *Massing & Site* tab>Modify Site panel, click

   (Property Line).
2. In the Create Property Line dialog box, select **Create by sketching**.
3. Use the Draw tools to create the property line and click

   (Finish Edit Mode).

- To edit sketched property lines, select a line, and in the *Modify | Property Lines* tab>Property Lines panel, select

  (Edit Sketch).

How To: Convert Sketched Property Lines to Table-Based Lines

1. Select the property line, and in the *Modify | Property Lines* tab>Property Lines panel, click (Edit Table).
2. In the Constraints Lost dialog box, read the message and click **Yes** or **No** to continue, as shown in Figure 2–33.
   - Once a sketched-base property line has been converted, it cannot go back to a sketch.

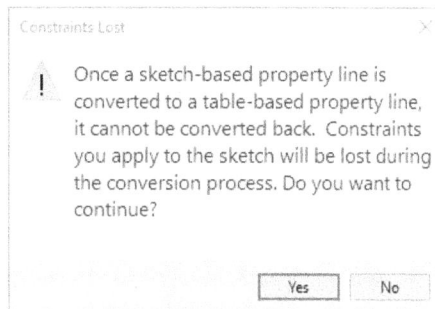

Constraints Lost

! Once a sketch-based property line is converted to a table-based property line, it cannot be converted back. Constraints you apply to the sketch will be lost during the conversion process. Do you want to continue?

Yes   No

Figure 2–33

Creating Building Pads

A building pad on a toposurface cuts or fills the surface around the area of the pad. You can create the pad from existing walls or sketch it with lines. The example in Figure 2–34 shows the site with a building pad in section.

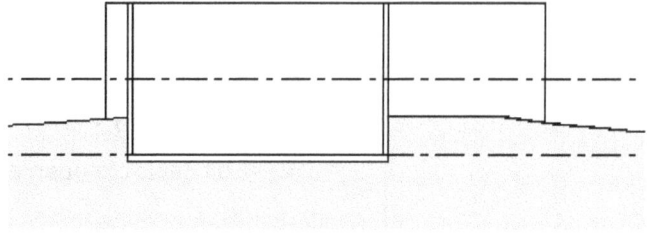

Figure 2–34

- A pad is an element in the project that might be in the same plane as a floor. When placing a pad, you will indicate what level it is starting from and any offsets from that level.

- A pad affects the surrounding surface and a floor element does not, meaning that a pad will cut out or fill in toposurface around any surrounding elements, whereas a floor will not.

- Building pads can only be added to toposurfaces from the site plan or, if needed, from a floor plan view.

  - If you cannot see your building pad in the view you are in, check your view's properties view range.

- Pads can be turned on or off in the Visibility/Graphic Overrides dialog box, under the *Site* category.

- The sketch of a pad must form a closed loop, but it can contain additional loops inside to display openings (such as a courtyard). Use the **Trim** and **Split** tools to ensure the lines create a closed loop. If you have several buildings, create a pad for each one.

You may need to toggle between visual styles, such as Wireframe, Hidden, and Shaded.

How To: Create a Building Pad

1. Open the site plan view with an existing toposurface. Building pads must be drawn on a toposurface.
2. In the *Massing & Site* tab>Model Site panel, click

   ▣ (Building Pad).
3. In the *Modify | Create Pad Boundary* tab>Draw panel, click

   ⌐ (Boundary Line). You can use any of the Draw tools or

   click ▨ (Pick Walls) to establish the outline of the building pad.

4. In Properties, specify a *Level* and a *Height Offset from Level* for the depth of the pad and set any phasing as needed.

    -   You can slope pads in one direction for drainage using

        (Slope Arrow).

5. Click (Finish Edit Mode).

-   To edit the building pad, click on the pad and in the *Modify |*

    Pads tab>Mode panel, select (Edit Boundary) to make modifications.

-   Just like with floors, you can create a new pad type and modify its layers, materials, and thickness.

Practice 2b

Add a Property Line and a Building Pad

Practice Objectives

- Create a property line by sketching.
- Add a building pad.

In this practice, you will add a property line and a building pad to a toposurface, as shown in Figure 2–35.

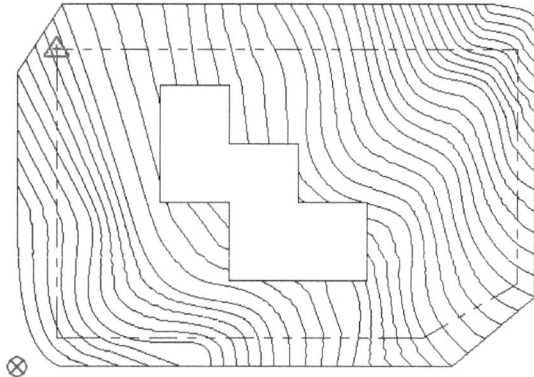

Figure 2–35

Task 1 - Create a property line.

1. In the practice files folder, open **New-Site-Pad-M.rvt**.

2. Ensure that you are in the **Floor Plans: Site** view.

3. In the *Massing & Site* tab>Modify Site panel, click
   (Property Line).

4. In the Create Property Line dialog box (as shown in Figure 2–36), select **Create by sketching**.

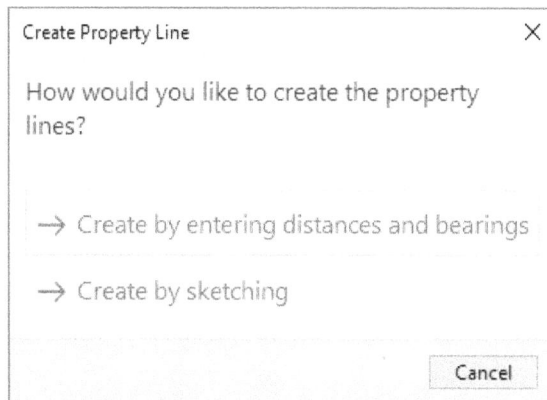

Figure 2–36

5. Sketch the property line, as shown in Figure 2–37.

   • Use the survey point as the start point of the property line.

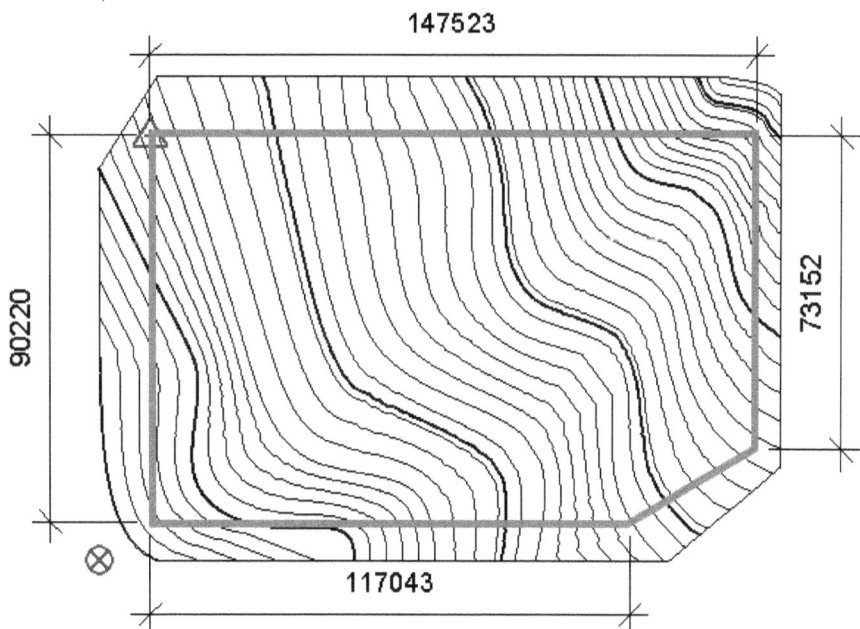

Figure 2–37

6. Click ✓ (Finish Edit Mode).

Task 2 - Create a building pad.

1. In the *Massing & Site* tab>Model Site panel, click
    ⬜ (Building Pad).

2. In the *Modify | Create Pad Boundary* tab>Draw panel, click
    ⎣ (Boundary Line). Use the Draw tools to establish the
    outline of the building pad, as shown in Figure 2–38.

    *   Use the survey point to identify the start point of the pad.
        Use reference planes and dimensions as needed.

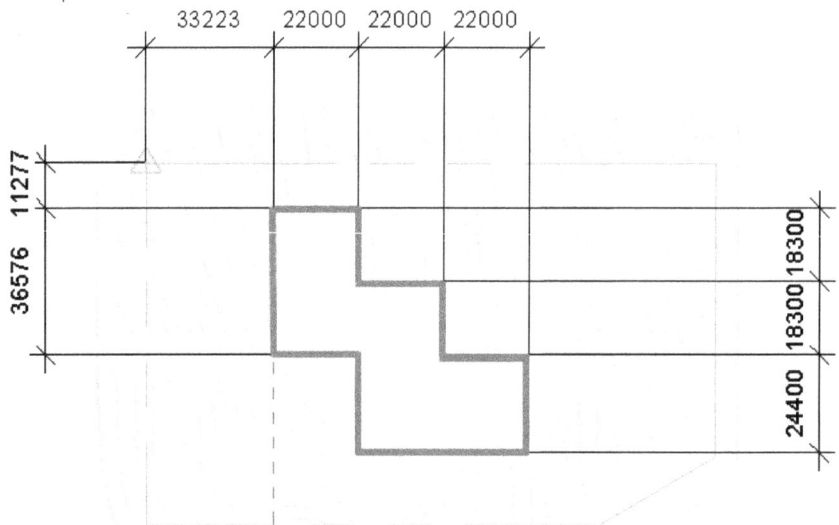

Figure 2–38

3. In Properties, verify that the *Level* is **Level 1** and the *Height
    Offset from Level* is set to **0**.

4. Click ✓ (Finish Edit Mode).

5. Open the **Site Section** view and see how the pad cuts the
    site, as shown in Figure 2–39.

Figure 2–39

6. Save and close the project.

2.3 Modifying Toposurfaces

Building a new structure requires that the earth around it be moved to make space for the building and to promote drainage. This means you need to modify the toposurface beyond just introducing the building pad and applying different materials, as shown in Figure 2–40. You can use commands to finalize the site design, such as **Subregion**, **Split Surface**, and **Graded Region**.

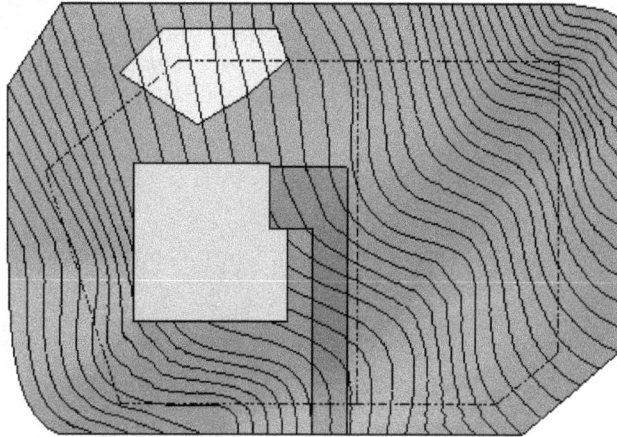

Figure 2–40

Creating Subregions

When you submit a preliminary proposal, you might want to display different materials on parts of the toposurface without changing the contours. You can quickly create subregions of the surface and apply different materials to them, as shown above in Figure 2–40.

*The subregions display with a boundary, but are still part of the main toposurface. Set the Visual Style to **Shaded**, **Consistent Colors**, or **Realistic** to display the colors of the materials.*

How To: Create a Subregion

1. In the *Massing & Site* tab>Modify Site panel, click ▧ (Subregion).
2. In the *Modify | Create Subregion Boundary* tab>Draw panel, use the Draw tools to outline the subregion.
3. In Properties, modify the *Material* for the subregion to show a different material, such as concrete to represent a sidewalk.
4. Click ✎ (Finish Edit Mode).
- The subregion is still selected. In Properties, specify a material if you did not do it before.

- To modify a subregion, select the subregion in the view and in the *Modify |Topography* tab>Subregion panel, click ⬚ (Edit Boundary).

- To remove a subregion, select it but do not edit the boundary. Press <Delete>.

Splitting Surfaces

⬚ (Split Surface) is a more powerful command that breaks toposurfaces into separate pieces. Each surface can be edited individually and be assigned different materials, as shown in Figure 2–41. Users can also name the various topographical surfaces within Properties.

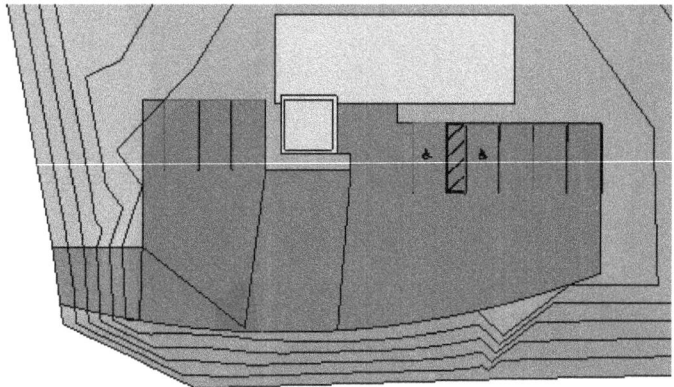

Figure 2–41

For example, you can break the topography into sections for parking areas, grassy areas, roadways, and sidewalks. You can also delete sections that you do not need in the project.

How To: Split a Surface

1. In the *Massing & Site* tab>Modify Site panel, click ⬚ (Split Surface).
2. Select the toposurface to split.
3. In the *Modify | Split Surface* tab>Draw panel, use the Draw tools to create a splitting boundary.
4. In Properties, modify the *Material* for the surface as needed.

5. Click ⬚ (Finish Edit Mode).

- The boundary does not need to be a closed object, but must split the surface into two pieces.

- To modify a split surface boundary, select the split surface and in the *Modify |Topography* tab>Subregion panel, click ⬚ (Edit Boundary).

How To: Merge Surfaces

1. In the *Massing & Site* tab>Modify Site panel, click 🔲 (Merge Surfaces).
2. Select the two adjacent surfaces that you want to merge.
   - If materials are applied to the surfaces, the new merged surface takes on the material of the first selected surface.

Grading a Site

The most time-consuming part of site work is deciding how to grade a site and adjusting the contours' elevations accordingly. You can make sections of the site flatter or steeper and you always need to verify that the drainage pattern flows away from the building and towards the storm drains. To make this process easier, use the ⬦ (Graded Region) command to create a proposed topography surface attached to the existing topography surface (from your selection), which automatically calculates the cut/fill and shows the area that will be demolished. Modify the location of points, then automatically demolish and add contours.

Refer to the ASCENT guide Autodesk Revit: Collaboration Tools for more information on phasing.

- When creating a graded region, it is best practice to place the existing toposurface on an existing phase. The graded region will automatically place itself on the New Construction phase which can be modified if other phases have been created.

- In Properties, set the *Phase Created* of the original toposurface to **Existing** (as shown in Figure 2–42) before starting the **Graded Region** command.

Phasing		≽
Phase Created	Existing	
Phase Demolished	None	

Figure 2–42

- When you modify topography with the **Graded Region** command, the software automatically calculates the *Cut* and *Fill* for the surface. This information is displayed in Properties (as shown in Figure 2–43) and can be added to a schedule.

Phasing		⋩
Phase Created	New Construction	
Phase Demolished	None	
Other		⋩
Net cut/fill	-910.956 m³	
Fill	0.993 m³	
Cut	911.949 m³	

Figure 2–43

How To: Grade a Site

1. Select the toposurface and, in Properties, verify that the *Phase Created* of the toposurface is set to **Existing**.
2. In the *Massing & Site* tab>Modify Site panel, click

   ⬆ (Graded Region).
3. The Edit Graded Region dialog box opens, as shown in Figure 2–44. Select how you want the new toposurface to be copied. You have the option of creating a replica of the original or an outline of the points.

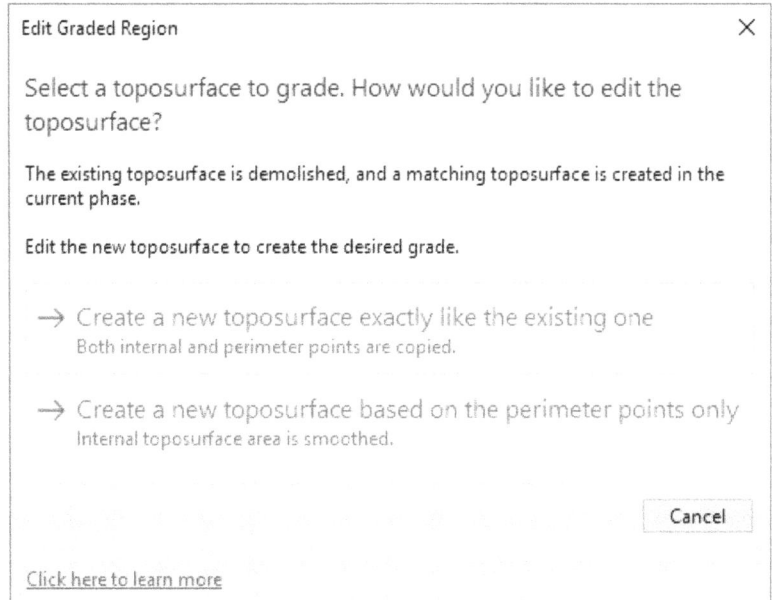

Edit Graded Region   ✕

Select a toposurface to grade. How would you like to edit the toposurface?

The existing toposurface is demolished, and a matching toposurface is created in the current phase.

Edit the new toposurface to create the desired grade.

→ Create a new toposurface exactly like the existing one
   Both internal and perimeter points are copied.

→ Create a new toposurface based on the perimeter points only
   Internal toposurface area is smoothed.

                                                            Cancel

Click here to learn more

Figure 2–44

4. Select the toposurface that you want to grade.

5. Modify the points in the surface:

- In the *Modify | Edit Surface* tab>Tools panel, click

  (Place Point) to add new points.

- Select a point and in the Options Bar, change the *Elevation*.

- Delete points that are no longer needed.

6. Click (Finish Surface).

- If the surface is open or there is a conflict, an alert box opens.

- If you are in a shaded view, the demolished area displays in red. Set the *Visual Style* to **Hidden** to display the contours and points more clearly.

Cut/Fill Volumes

You can track cut and fill volumes of the graded region and pad elements in the project and report them in a topography schedule. For this to work, you must first ensure the toposurface you are working with is set to an existing. The graded region will be placed in the **New Construction** phase. Note that the cut and fill calculations are an approximate result with an accuracy of +/- 1% to 2%.

2.4 Annotating Site Plans

Site plan annotation can include information about setbacks, dimensions, and spaces for the various site components, utility and grading information, etc. Most of this information can be added with standard tools, such as **Text** and **Dimensions**. There are several annotation items that work with site plans: **Label Contours** (shown in Figure 2–45), **Spot Elevation**, and **Spot Coordinate**.

Label Contours only works with toposurfaces.

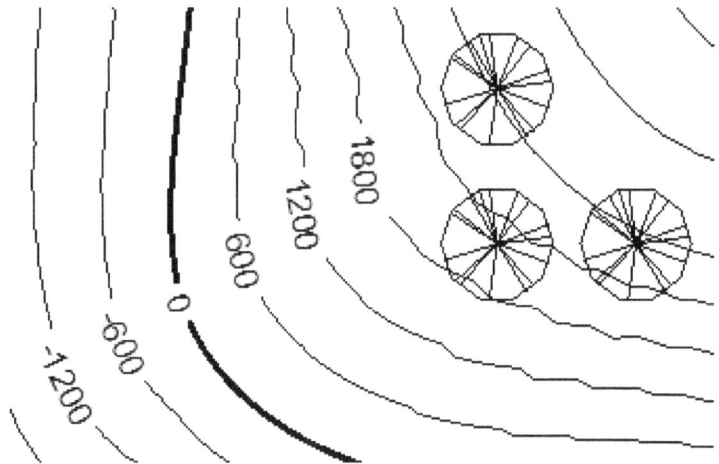

Figure 2–45

Labeling Contours

Labeling the contours can help the process of grading regions by displaying the level of the contour lines in the region in which you are working.

How To: Label Contours

1. Make sure you are in a plan view as contour labels are not available to use in any other view.

2. In the *Massing & Site* tab>Modify Site panel, click ^50^ (Label Contours).

3. Draw a line across the contours that you want to label.

4. Continue drawing as many lines as needed.

How To: Modify Contour Labels' Elevation Base

You can specify which coordinates your contour labels are reading from based on the project base point, based on the survey point, or relative to a level.

1. Select a contour line. In Properties, select **Edit Type**.
2. In the Type Properties dialog box, set the *Elevation Base* to the required value. Figure 2–46 shows the three options you can choose from.

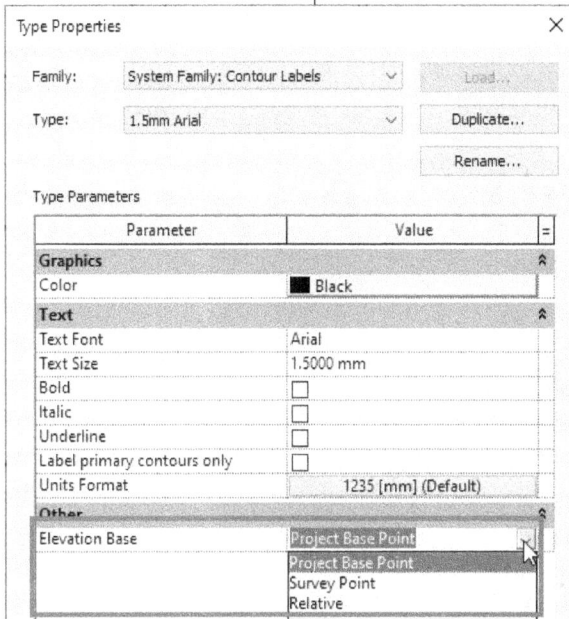

Figure 2–46

- **Project Base Point:** If *Elevation Base* is set to **Project Base Point**, the elevation displayed will be reflecting the project's internal origin.

- **Survey Point:** This option will display the elevations based off of the survey point location.

- **Relative:** This option displays the elevations relative to a floor plan, which you can specify in the Relative Base drop-down list in the instance properties, as shown in Figure 2–47.

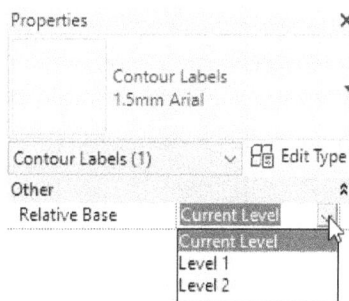

Figure 2–47

Add Spot Dimensions

The spot dimensioning tools display important information about specific points on your toposurface, as shown in Figure 2–48.

 (Spot Elevation) gathers the elevation information from a selected point, while (Spot Coordinate) gathers the coordinate information for a point. You can also modify where the spot elevation and spot coordinate reference from with respect to project base point, survey point, internal point, or relative to a level.

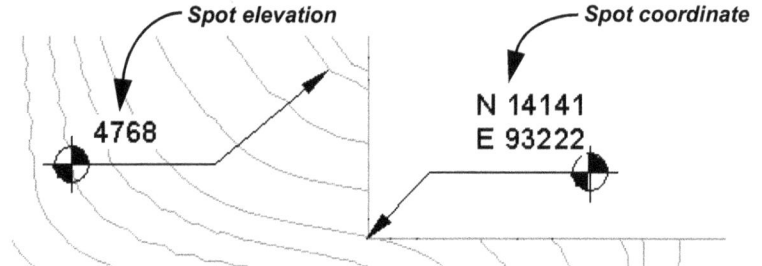

Figure 2–48

- Spot dimensions can be added on any type of model element, not just toposurfaces.

How To: Add Spot Elevations/Coordinates

1. In the *Annotate* tab>Dimension panel, click (Spot Elevation) or (Spot Coordinate).
2. In the Type Selector, select the type that you want to use from the list, as shown in Figure 2–49 for spot elevations.

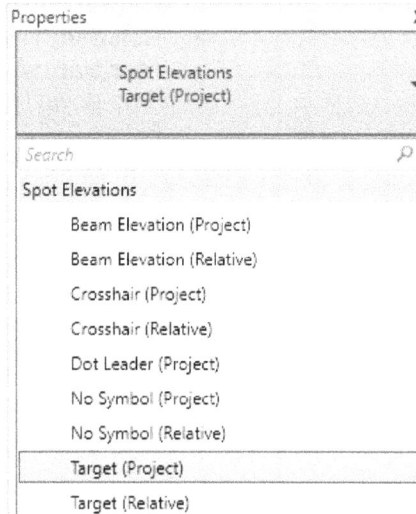

Figure 2–49

3. In the Options Bar, select the **Leader** and **Shoulder** options. The spot coordinate Options Bar also includes a list of *Display Elevations* to select from, as shown in Figure 2–50.

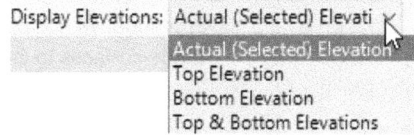

Figure 2–50

4. Select a point to dimension and place the leader line and target or text. The software automatically gathers the information from the selected point.

   • The value of the spot dimension displays as you move the cursor over the site.

5. Click ⌖ (Modify) to end the command.

How To: Modify the Spot Coordinates' Base

1. Select a spot coordinate, and in Properties, select **Edit Type**.
2. In the Type Properties dialog box, in the *Constraints* section, set the *Coordinate Base* to **Survey Point**, **Project Base Point**, or **Internal Origin**, as shown in Figure 2–51.

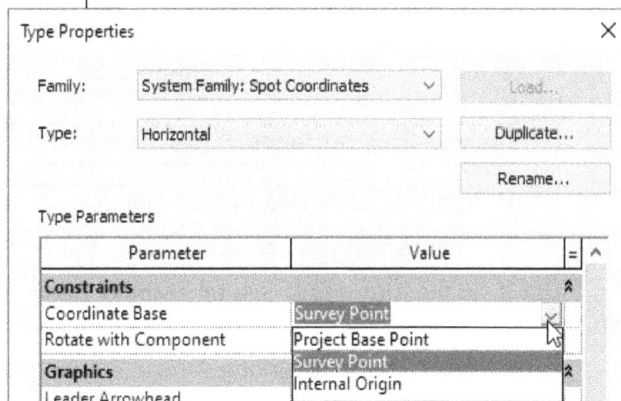

Figure 2–51

How To: Modify the Spot Elevations' Base

1. Select a spot elevation and in Properties, select **Edit Type**.
2. In the Type Properties dialog box, in the *Constraints* section, set the *Elevation Base* to **Survey Point**, **Project Base Point**, or **Relative**.

Practice 2c

Modify Toposurfaces

Practice Objectives

- Split surfaces and change the material of an existing toposurface.
- Grade surfaces to create an even patio with a sunken pool.
- Grade the slope of the parking area and driveway.

In this practice, you will add several new surfaces, label the contour lines to prepare contours for modification, and modify the points within a graded region, as shown in Figure 2–52.

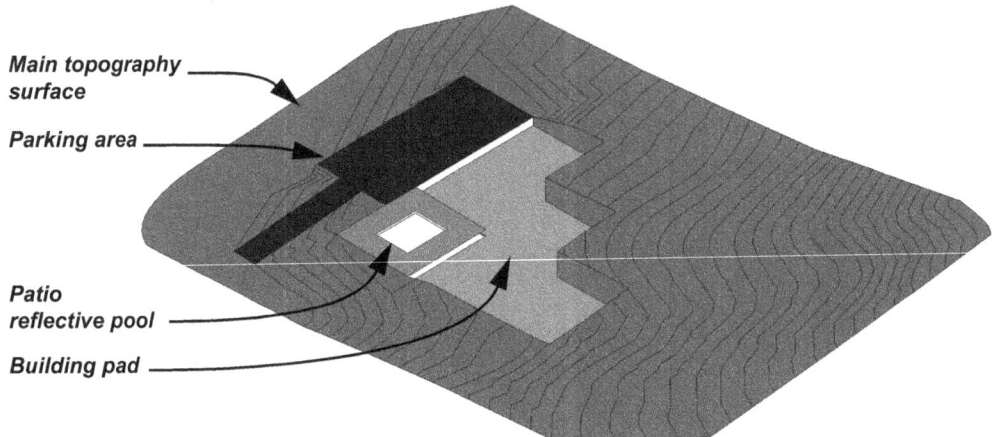

Main topography surface

Parking area

Patio reflective pool

Building pad

Figure 2–52

Task 1 - Split surfaces.

1. In the practice files folder, open **New-Site-Modify-M.rvt**.

2. Ensure that you are in the **Floor Plans: Site** view.

3. In the *Massing & Site* tab>Modify Site panel, click (Split Surface).

4. Select the toposurface.

Note: Throughout the practice, you may need to toggle between the Hidden Line and Shaded visual styles for the view.

5. Draw the boundary for the patio, as shown in Figure 2–53. (Hint: Use the rectangle draw tool.)

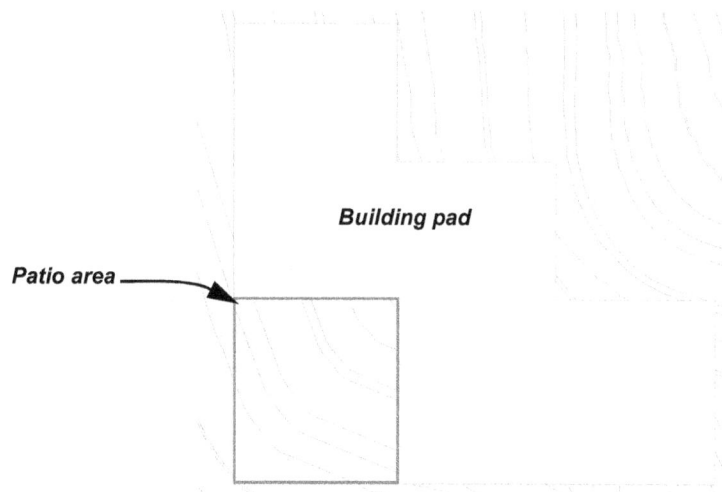

Building pad

Patio area ————→

Figure 2–53

6. In the *Modify | Split Surface* tab>Mode panel, click

   (Finish Edit Mode).

7. Click in an empty area in the view to clear the selection.

8. Start the **Split Surface** command again, but this time select the patio surface area that was just created.

9. Use the rectangle draw tool and from the Options Bar, set the *Offset* to (negative) **-6000mm**. Select opposite corners of the patio and reflective pool area.

10. Click ✎ (Finish Edit Mode). There are now two surfaces, as shown in Figure 2–54.

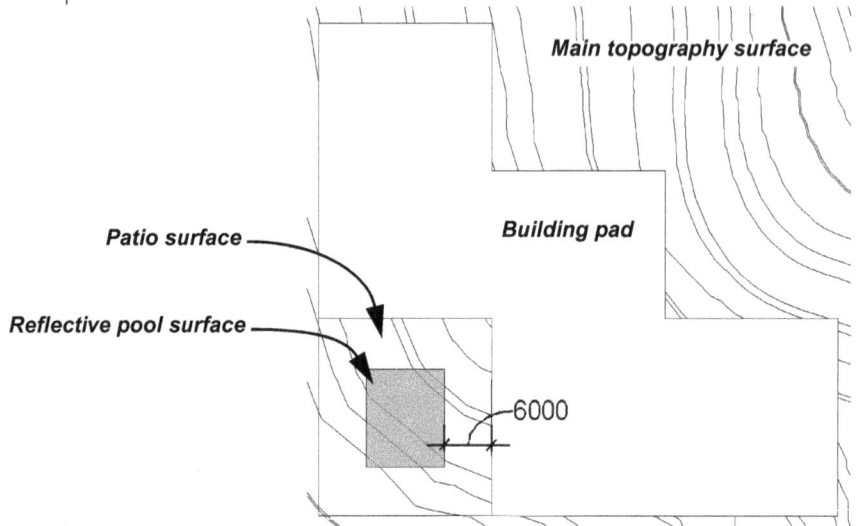

Main topography surface

Patio surface

Building pad

Reflective pool surface

-6000

Figure 2–54

11. Click in an empty area in the view to clear the selection.

12. Start the **Split Surface** command and select the main topography surface. Create the surface for the parking area, as shown in Figure 2–55. (Note: The main site in the image has been grayed out and dimensioned for clarity.)

13. Click ✎ (Finish Edit Mode).

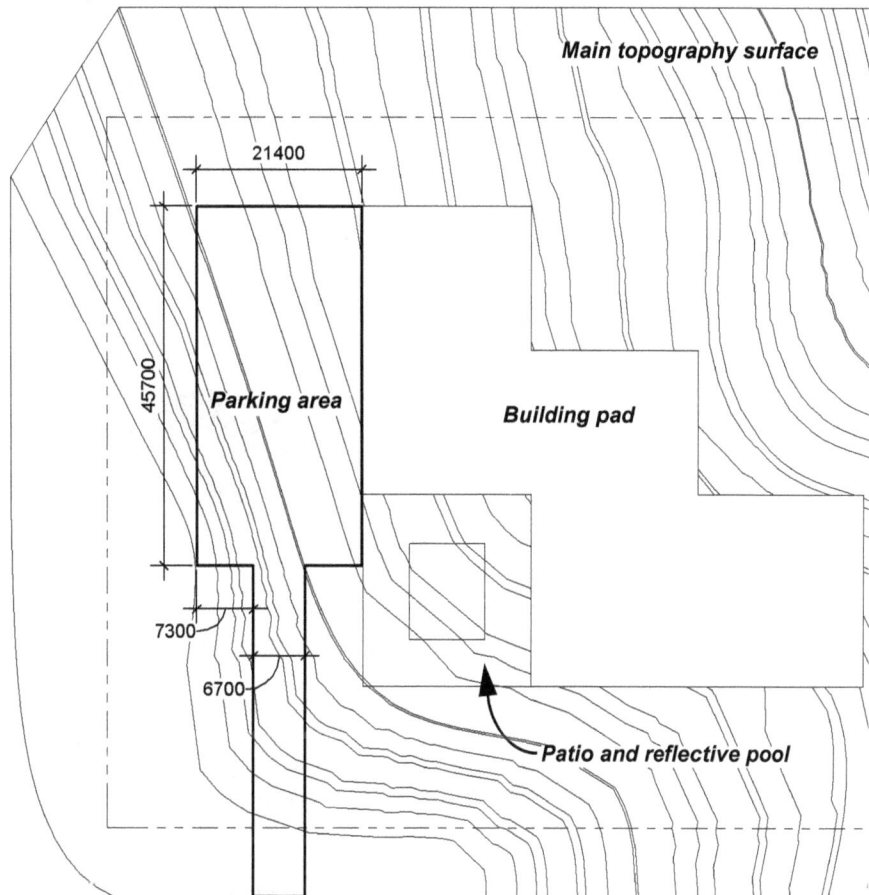

Figure 2–55

14. Click ▷ (Modify).

15. Save the project.

Task 2 - Apply materials.

---

1. Still in the **Site** view, from the View Control Bar, change the *Visual Style* to **Shaded**. The surfaces should all be brown except for the building pad.

2. Select the main topography surface. In Properties, under the *Materials and Finishes* section, click (browse) next to *Material*, as shown in Figure 2–56.

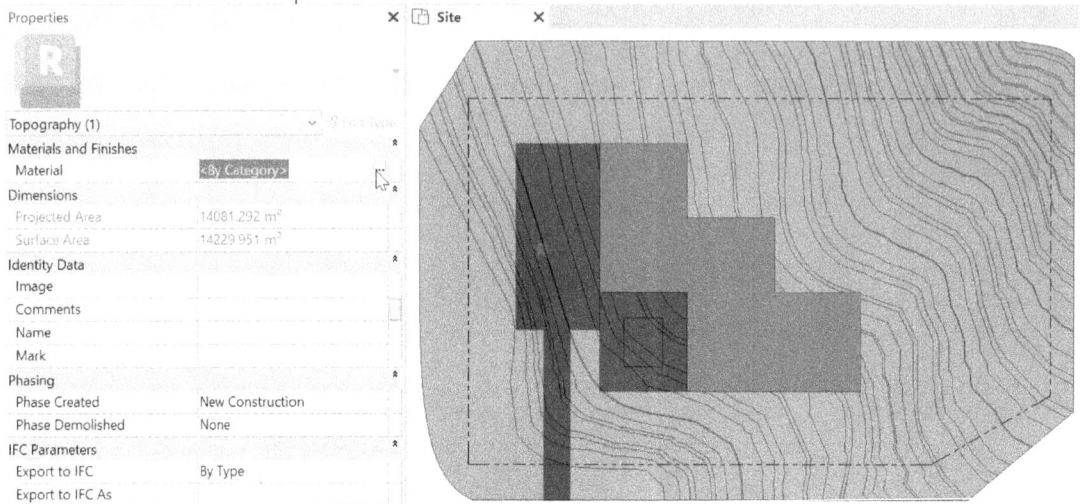

Figure 2–56

3. In the Material Browser dialog box, search for **grass**, then select **Grass** from the *Project Materials* list. On the *Graphics* tab, in the *Shading* section, check the checkbox for **Use Render Appearance**, as shown in Figure 2–57.

    *   If the material does not display in the *Project Materials* list, add it to the project from the *Library Materials* list. Click (Add to Document) to add the material to the project, as shown in Figure 2–57.

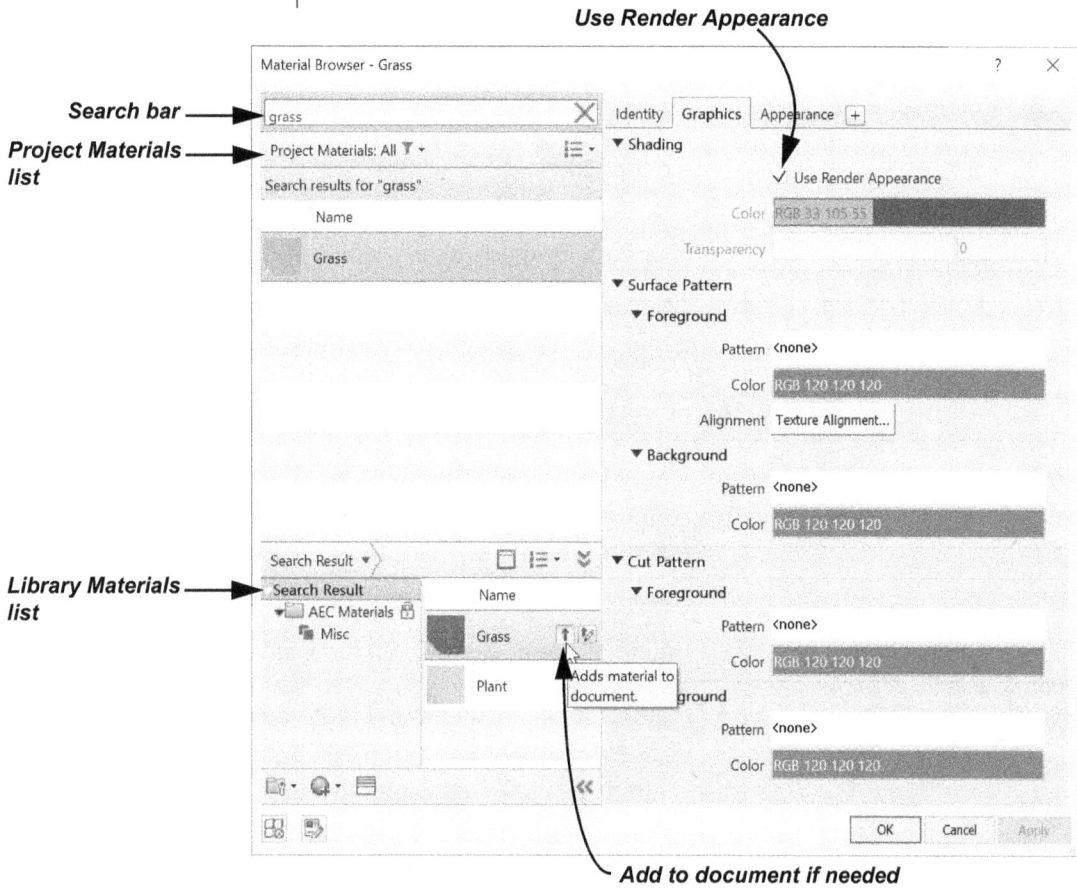

Use Render Appearance

Search bar ⟶

Project Materials list ⟶

Library Materials list ⟶

Add to document if needed

Figure 2–57

4. Click **OK**.

5. Click in an empty area in the view to clear the selection.

6. Continue to select and apply material to the rest of the surfaces, as follows:

   • Parking area: **Asphalt, Pavement**
   • Patio: **Stone, Natural Soldier**
   • Reflecting pool: **Water**

7. Switch the *Visual Style* to **Wireframe**.

8. Save the project.

Task 3 - Set phase and grade the surfaces.

1. Select all of the topography surfaces. (Hint: Select everything in the drawing and use ▽ (Filter) to filter out everything but the topography.)

2. In Properties, set the *Phase Created* to **Existing**. This is important for grading the surfaces.

3. Click in an empty area in the view to clear the selection.

4. Zoom in on the patio.

5. In the *Massing & Site* tab>Modify Site panel, click ⟁ (Graded Region).

6. In the Edit Graded Region dialog box, select **Create a new toposurface exactly like the existing one**.

7. Select the patio surface.

To select more than one point at a time, draw a window around them.

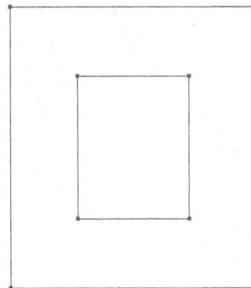

8. Delete all the points on both the inside and outside, except those on the corners of the patio and the corners of the pool (eight in total), as shown in Figure 2–58. This flattens the patio surface.

   • Hint: Turn off **Thin Lines** to see all the points, if needed.

Figure 2–58

9. Select the remaining eight corner points. In the Options Bar, set the *Elevation* to **2440mm**.

10. In the *Modify | Edit Surface* tab>Surface panel, click 🖋 (Finish Surface).

11. Start the **Graded Region** command again.

12. In the Edit Graded Region dialog box, select **Create a new toposurface exactly like the existing one**.

13. Select the reflective pool surface.

14. Delete the extra points and set the *Elevation* of the corner points of the pool to **1830mm**.

15. In the *Modify | Edit Surface* tab>Surface panel, click

    (Finish Surface) and save the project.

16. With nothing selected, in Properties, change the *Phase Filter* to **Show Complete**. This helps you to see which areas you have graded because the graded surfaces will not display contour lines going through the surface, as shown in Figure 2–59.

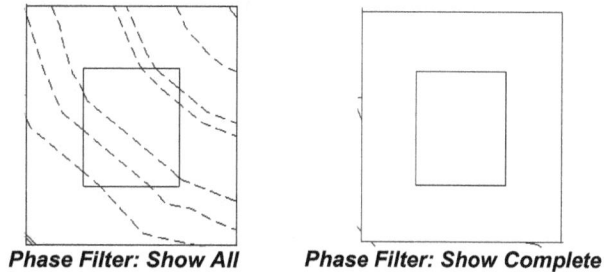

Phase Filter: Show All   *Phase Filter: Show Complete*

Figure 2–59

17. Start the **Graded Region** command again and select **Create a new toposurface exactly like the existing one**.

18. Select the parking area. Delete all of the points except the eight corner points, as shown in Figure 2–60.

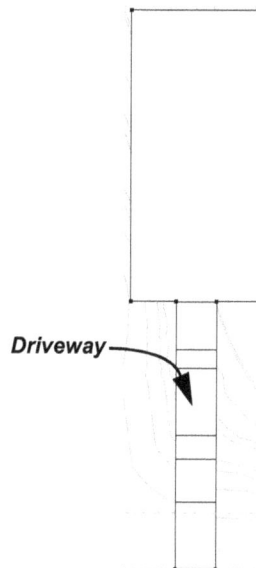

Driveway

Figure 2–60

19. Set the top six points of the parking area to **2440mm** and the bottom two points (driveway) to **0mm**. This creates a sloped driveway.

20. Click ✎ (Finish Surface) when you are finished.

21. Start the **Graded Region** command again and select **Create a new toposurface exactly like the existing one**. Select

    the main toposurface and click ✎ (Finish Surface). (You will not delete any points.)

22. Open up the 3D view. Set the *Visual Style* to **Consistent Colors**. The areas that are being removed display in red.

23. In Properties, change the *Phase Filter* to **Show Complete** to see the different surfaces and materials, as shown in Figure 2–61.

Figure 2–61

Task 4 - Modify topographical surfaces.

1. Return to the *Site* floor plan view. Select the building pad. Hint: While watching the Status Bar, press <Tab> to toggle through the surfaces until you see **Pads: Pad: Building Pad**, then click to select it.

2. In the *Modify | Pad* tab>Model panel, select ✐ (Edit Boundary).

3. In the *Modify Pads>Edit Boundary* tab>Draw panel, select
    (Slope Arrow). Place the slope arrow as shown in
    Figure 2–62, from one side of the building pad to the other.

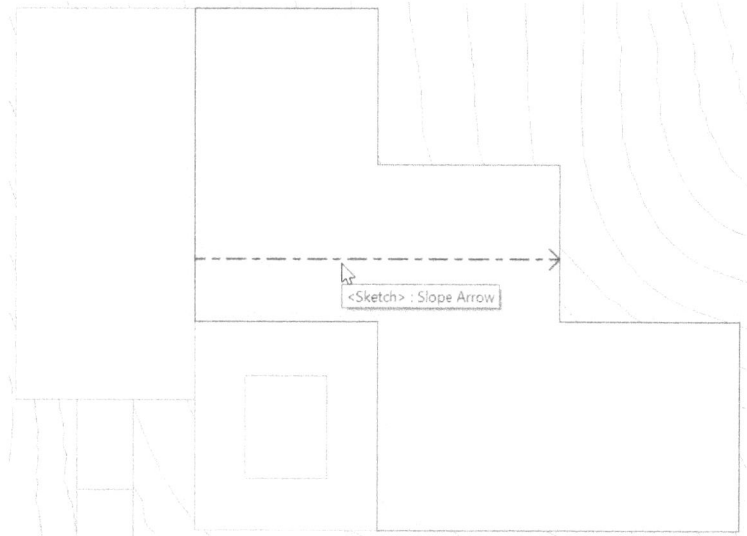

> `<Sketch> : Slope Arrow`

Figure 2–62

4. Click (Modify).

5. You want the pad to slope towards the parking area. Select
    the slope arrow and in Properties, under *Constraints*, change
    the *Specify* value to **Slope** using the drop-down list.

6. Under the *Dimensions* section, type **2%** for the *Slope* value
    and press <Enter>. Be sure you add the percent symbol (%).
    The percentage slope will change to the default rise/run
    value, as shown in Figure 2–63.

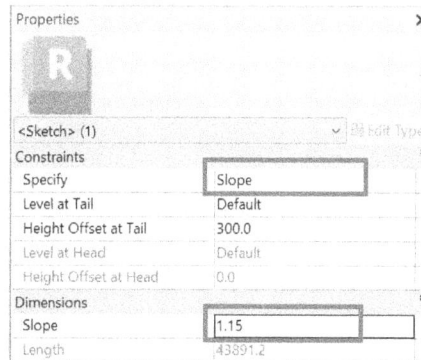

Figure 2–63

7. Click ✔ (Finish Edit Boundary) when you are finished.

8. Click ⌖ (Modify).

9. With just the **Site** and **3D** views open, type **WT** to tile the views side by side. Type **ZA** to zoom all for both views.

10. In the **Site** view, select the main grass topography surface.

11. In the *Modify | Topography* tab>Surface panel, click 📐 (Edit Surface).

12. Zoom in to the parking area and driveway.

13. Delete all the points along the parking area and driveway, as shown in Figure 2–64. Do not delete the parking area and driveway corner points or the northwest corner of the patio, as marked in the Figure 2–64.

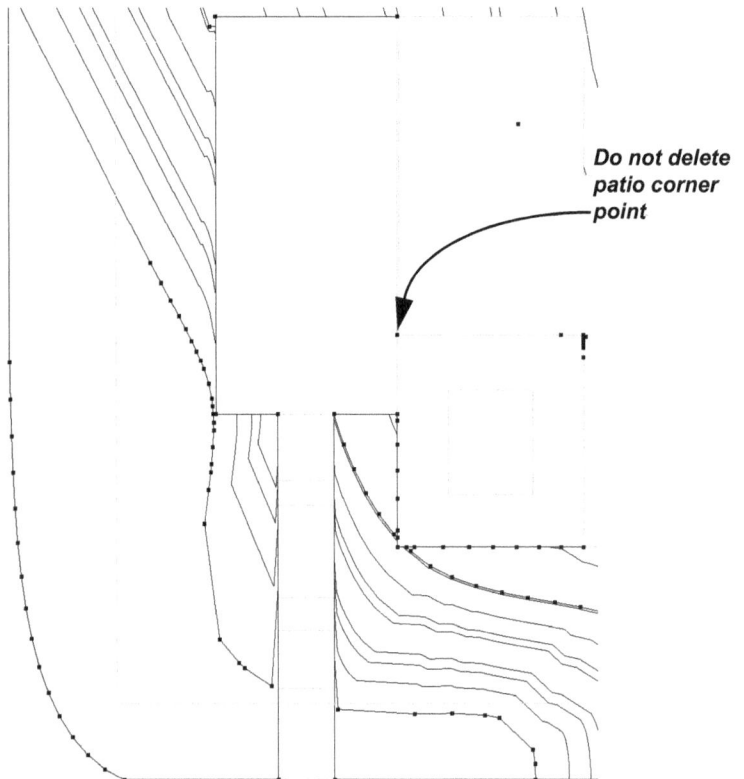

Figure 2–64

14. Change the elevations of the remaining points to **2440mm**. Select the two bottom corner points of the driveway and change them to **0mm**.

15. Zoom in to the patio area. Delete all points except for the corner points, making sure not to delete the corner point of the parking area, as shown in Figure 2–65. Change the elevation of the patio corner points to **2440mm**.

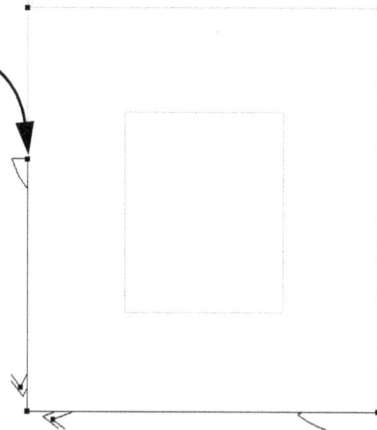

Do not delete parking area corner point

Figure 2–65

16. Click ✎ (Finish Edit Boundary) when you are finished.

17. Review the topography in the 3D view, as shown in Figure 2–66.

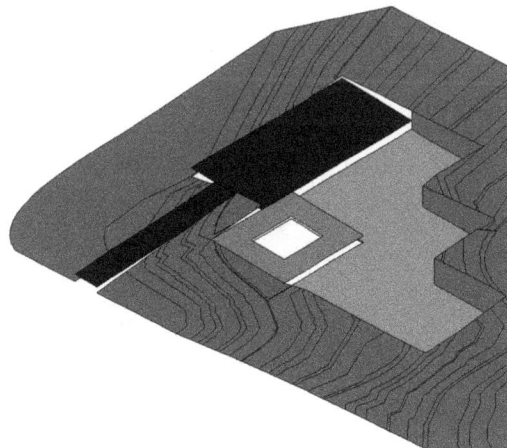

Figure 2–66

18. Save the project.

Task 5 - Add annotations

In this task, you will add contour labels and spot elevations to the topographies.

1. Return to the **Site** view, as contour labels are not available to use in any other view. Type **TW** to tab the views.

2. Change the scale to **1: 500**.

3. In the *Massing & Site* tab>Modify Site panel, click $^{\nearrow 50}$ (Label Contours). In the Options Bar, verify **Chain** is unchecked.

4. Draw three lines across the contours that you want to label, similar to those highlighted in Figure 2–67.

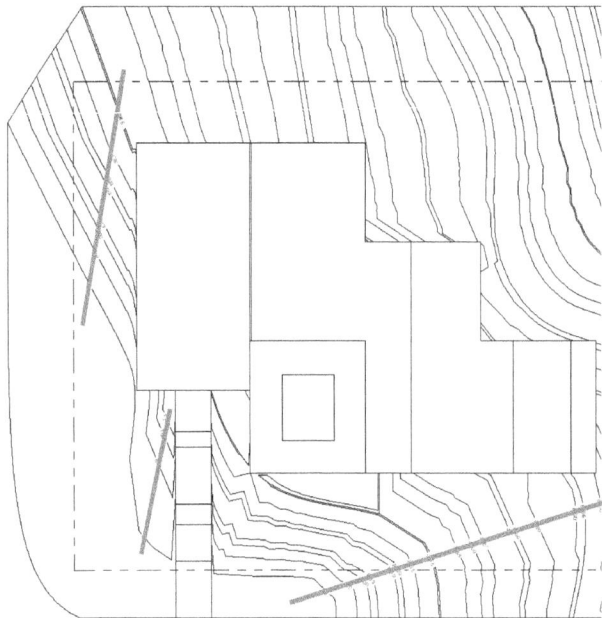

Figure 2–67

5. Select one of the contour labels you just created. The entire label line gets selected. In Properties, select **Edit Type**.

6. In the Type Properties dialog box, in the *Other* section, note that the *Elevation Base* is currently set to **Project Base**, as shown in Figure 2–68. Expand the *Elevation Base* value and select **Survey Point**.

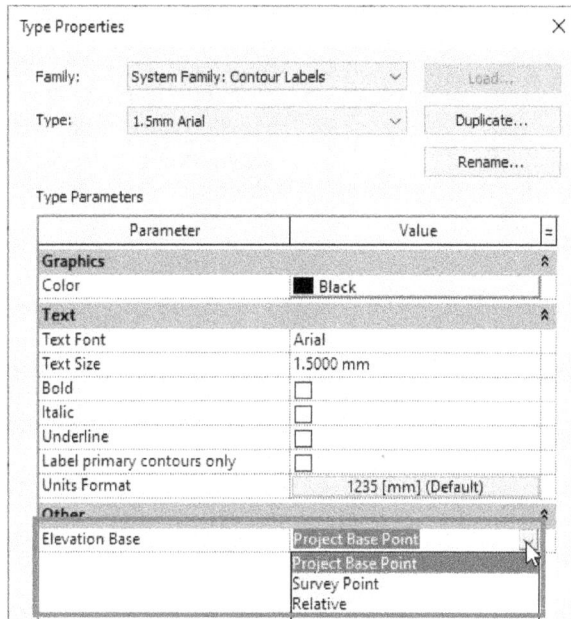

Figure 2–68

7. Click **Apply**. All contour labels update with the survey (sea level) elevations. This is because the *Elevation Base* is a type property of the contour labels.

8. Repeat the process to change the *Elevation Base* to **Relative** and click **OK**. All contour labels update to relative elevations, which by default is the current level.

9. Click (Modify).

10. Select a contour label. In Properties, change the *Relative Base* to **Level 2** and click **Apply.**

- Note that just the selected contour labels for that line now display values relative to the second level, whereas the other labels still reflect the **Current Level** elevations. This is because the *Relative Base* is a instance property.

11. Click (Modify).

12. In the *Annotate* tab>Dimension panel, select (Spot Elevation).

- Note that as you hover over various topographies or building pads or other surfaces, the reading of the unplaced spot elevation updates to reflect the current elevation.

13. Pick a point near the northwest corner of the parking area to place the spot elevation.

14. Continue to place spot elevations on the patio, pool, and building pad. Note that if you place more than one spot elevation on the building pad, the elevation will vary since it is sloped.

15. Click ⟋ (Modify).

16. In the *Annotate* tab>Dimension panel, select ⬜ (Spot Slope).

17. In Properties, select **Edit Type**.

18. In the Type Properties dialog box, in the *Primary Units* section, click the button to open the Format dialog box. Change the *Units* to **Percentage** and set the *Unit symbol* to %, as shown in Figure 2–69. Click **OK** twice.

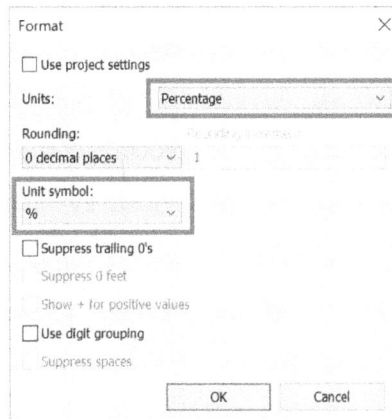

Figure 2–69

19. Hover your cursor over different surfaces. Note that the slope value changes or displays *[No Slope]*. Click to place a spot slope on the building pad and driveway.

20. Click ⟋ (Modify).

21. The final annotations should be similar to those shown in Figure 2–70.

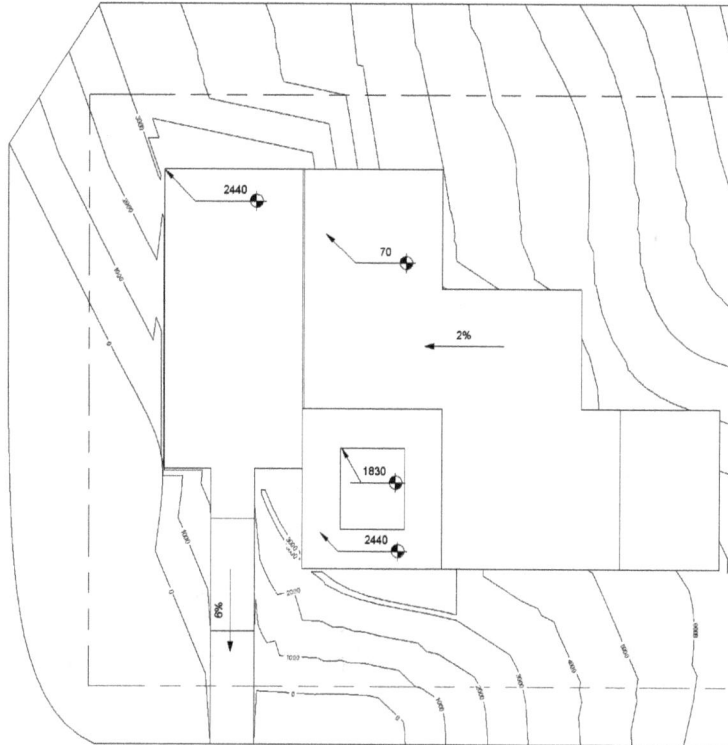

Figure 2–70

22. Save the project.

Task 6 - Add a topography schedule of the grass.

In this task, you will create a topography schedule in order to determine the cut/fill volume for the grass and the building pad.

1. In the *View* tab>Create panel, expand **Schedules** and select (Schedules/Quantities).

2. In the New Schedule dialog box, select **Topography** from the *Category* list, as shown in Figure 2–71. Click **OK**.

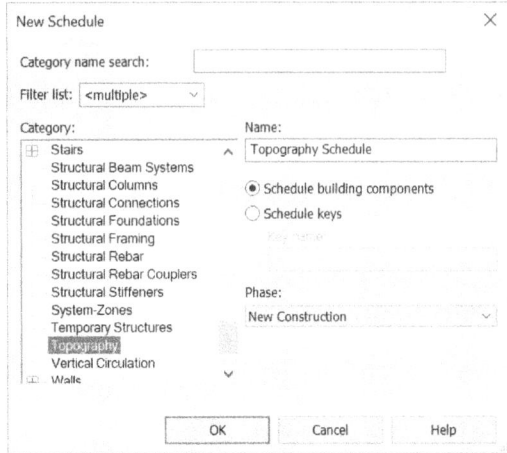

Figure 2–71

3. In the Schedule Properties dialog box, on the *Fields* tab, select the following *Available fields*: **Name**, **Cut**, **Fill**, **Net cut/fill**, as shown in Figure 2–72.

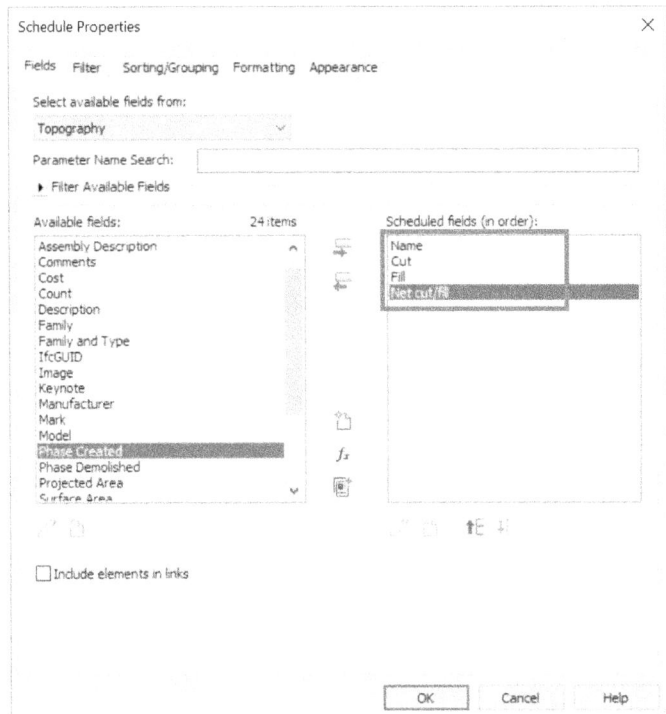

Figure 2–72

4. On the *Sorting/Grouping* tab, select **Grand Totals**.

5. On the *Formatting* tab, in the *Fields* area, select **Net cut/fill**. Choose **Calculate totals** from the Field formatting drop-down list, as shown in Figure 2–73.

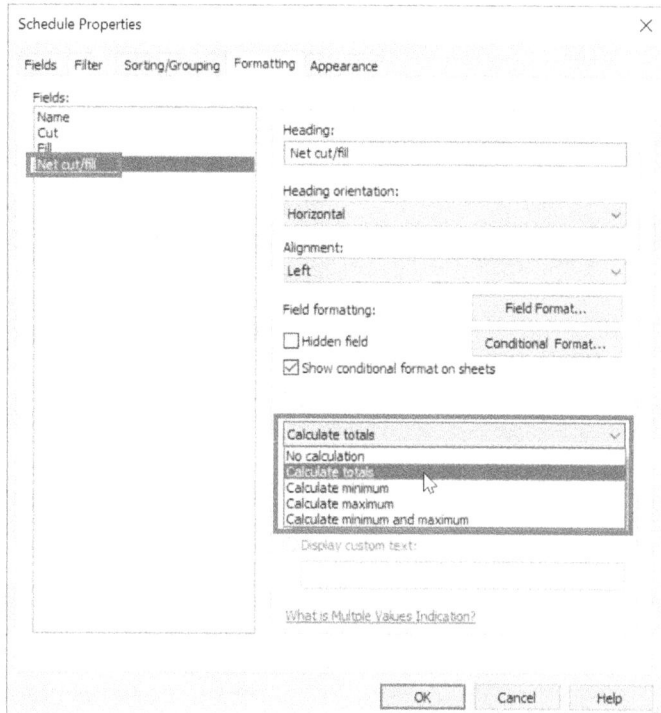

Figure 2–73

6. Click **OK**.

*Note: Your values may differ from the values shown in the schedule depending on your surface grading. If your values show all zeros, you need to make sure all of your toposurfaces are set to the **Existing** phase created.*

7. You schedule will populate, as shown in Figure 2–74. Note that only the grass and building pad show cut/fill values.

<Topography Schedule>			
A	B	C	D
Name	Cut	Fill	Net cut/fill
	209.17 m^3	130.48 m^3	-78.69 m^3
	12864.54 m^3	0.00 m^3	-12864.54 m^3
Grand total: 5			-12943.23 m^3

Figure 2–74

8. To filter out the fields that are empty or have zero values, in Properties, click **Edit...** next to *Filter*.

9. Set the *Filter by:* to **Cut** > **has a value**, as shown in Figure 2–75. Click **OK**.

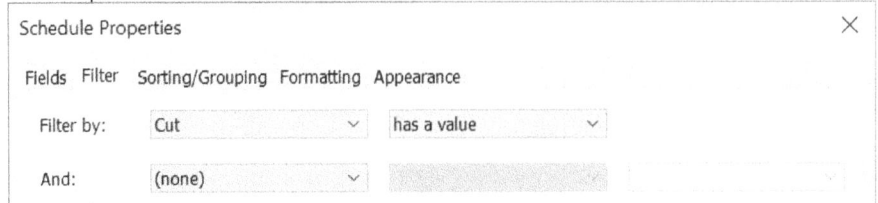

Schedule Properties				✕

Fields Filter Sorting/Grouping Formatting Appearance

Filter by:	Cut ⌄	has a value ⌄	
And:	(none) ⌄		⌄

Figure 2–75

10. The schedule will update to display only the grass and the building pad rows. Note that the *Name* column is blank and you will need to manually specify names for these rows. In the *Name* column, type **Grass** for the first row and **Building Pad** for the second row, as shown in Figure 2–76. How you adjusted the grade regions will determine what values will be reported in the schedule.

<Topography Schedule>			
A	**B**	**C**	**D**
wt	Cut	Fill	Net cut/fill
Grass	209.17 m³	130.48 m³	-78.69 m³
Building Pad	12864.54 m³	0.00 m³	-12864.54 m³
Grand total: 2			-12943.23 m³

Figure 2–76

11. Save and close the project.

2.5 Adding Site Components

When you have established a site with surfaces and building pads, you can populate it with other site elements, such as parking spaces and trees. Site components are inserted like any other component. However, instead of taking on the current level when they are inserted, they link to the elevation of the contour where they are placed, as shown in Figure 2–77.

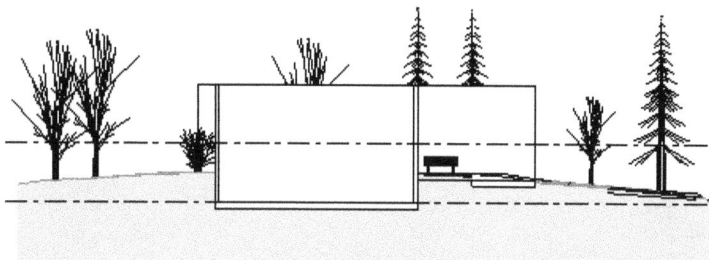

Figure 2–77

* To access site components, click ⬙ (Site Component) or
  ▦ (Parking Component) in the *Massing & Site* tab>Model Site panel.

* To load different types of components, in the *Modify | Parking Component* or *Site Component* tab>Mode panel, click
  ⬙ (Load Family).

* The Autodesk Revit family library includes the *Site* folder with sub-folders for *Accessories*, *Logistics*, *Parking*, and *Utilities*.
  * *Accessories* include items such as building signs.
  * *Logistics* includes trucks, cranes, and other construction equipment.
  * *Parking* includes parking spaces, islands, direction arrows, and an ADA-compliant curb, parking space, and symbol.
  * *Utilities* includes catch basins, fire hydrants, manhole covers, and more.

* Additional trees and shrubs can be loaded from the Revit Library's *Planting* folder. Each family (Shrub, Conifer, and Deciduous) contains a variety of types and heights of trees.

- Many components, not just site-specific components, are face-based and can use a toposurface as a host if they are added in a view in which the toposurface is visible.

- You can choose a new host for the component/site component by clicking ![icon](Pick New Host) (Pick New Host) in the associated *Modify* tab>Host panel, and verifying that the component is associated with the correct surface. If **Pick Host** does not work, change the elevation of the component in Properties.

Practice 2d | Add Site Components

Practice Objective

• Add trees, parking spaces, and the ADA symbol to a toposurface.

In this practice, you will add parking spaces, ADA symbols, and trees, as shown in Figure 2–78.

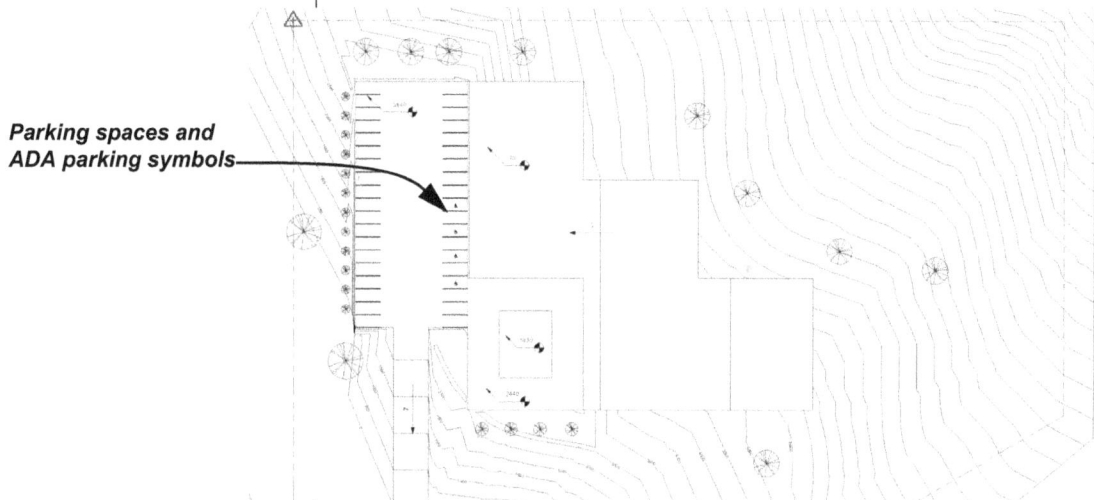

Parking spaces and
ADA parking symbols

Figure 2–78

Task 1 - Add site components.

1. In the practice files folder, open
   New-Site-Components-M.rvt.

2. Ensure that you are in the **Floor Plans: Site** view.

3. In the *Insert* tab>Load from Library panel, click (Load Family).

4. In the Load Family dialog box, navigate to the practice files
   Families folder and select **M_Parking Space.rfa** and
   M_Parking Symbol - ADA.rfa. Click **Open**.

5. In the *Massing & Site* tab>Model Site panel, click

   ▭ (Parking Component) and place the **4800 x 2400mm - 90 deg** parking spaces as shown in Figure 2–79.

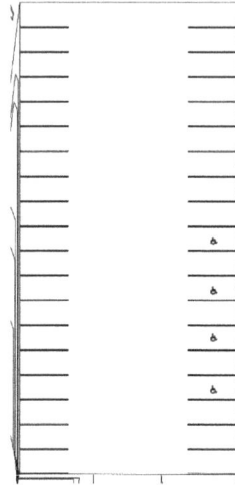

Figure 2–79

6. In the *Massing & Site* tab>Model Site panel, click 🌲 (Site Component) and place the **ADA symbol** within the parking spaces.

7. Continue using the **Site Component** command and add trees around the property using various types and heights.

8. Add other components. These can include site accessories, such as bollards and planters, or parking symbols, such as direction arrows.

Task 2 - View the completed model.

1. Open a 3D view and set the *Visual Style* to **Shaded**, then switch to **Realistic** to see the different visual styles.

2. In Properties, set the *Phase Filter* to **Show Complete**.

3. Rotate the 3D view.

4. You can also add retaining walls or other building features.

5. Save and close the project.

Chapter Review Questions

1. In which of the following ways can you NOT create topographical surfaces, such as that shown in Figure 2–80?

    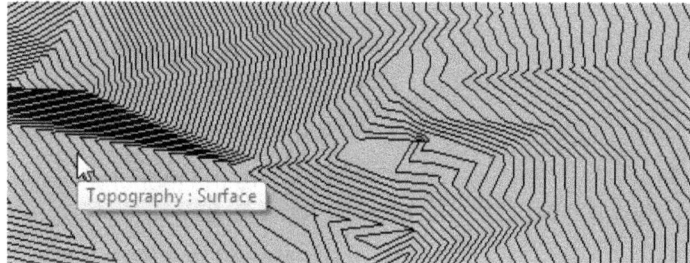

    Figure 2–80

    a. From an imported drawing that was creating using the AutoCAD® software.

    b. By sketching.

    c. From a family file.

    d. From a points file.

2. Which of the following commands enables you to modify a toposurface so that you can change various parts of the surface to different materials (as shown in Figure 2–81) and modify the contours separately from the main toposurface?

    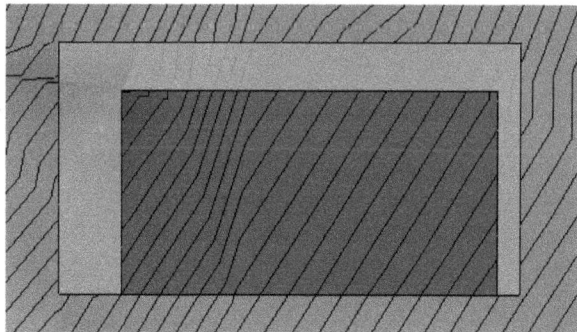

    Figure 2–81

    a. Edit Surface

    b. Graded Region

    c. Merge Surface

    d. Split Surface

3. Which of the following best describes the difference between a building pad and a floor?

   a. A pad affects the surrounding surface and a floor element does not.

   b. A pad must be placed at a level and a floor can be placed above or below a level.

   c. A pad must line up with walls and a floor can also be sketched.

   d. A pad cannot be sloped and a floor can be sloped.

4. Why are the topography lines dashed and displayed in red in Figure 2–82?

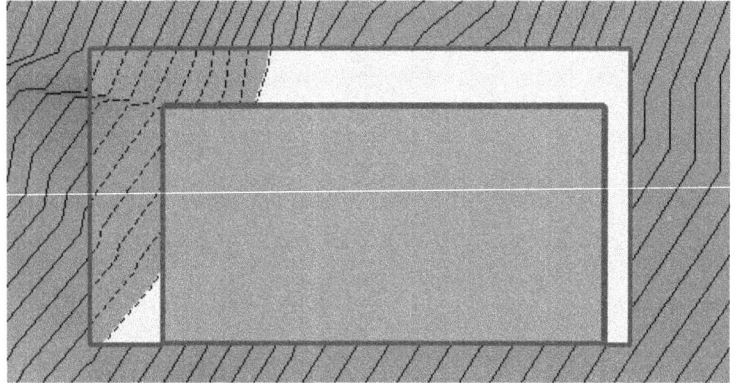

Figure 2–82

   a. The toposurface has been edited.

   b. The toposurface has been graded.

   c. The toposurface is set to Existing.

   d. The toposurface has been split.

5. Which of the following annotations is most helpful when you are modifying the grading of a toposurface?

   a. Label Contours

   b. Spot Elevation

   c. Spot Coordinate

   d. Linear Dimension

6. Which of the following is most likely true about the tree shown on the left in Figure 2–83?

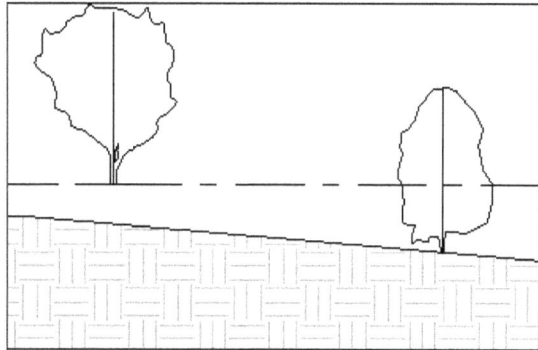

Figure 2–83

   a. It is not a site component.

   b. It is hosted by level.

   c. It has been moved off the surface.

   d. It has been offset above the surface.

Command Summary

Button	Command	Location
Toposurfaces		
	Building Pad	• **Ribbon:** *Massing & Site* tab>Model Site panel
	Edit Boundary	• **Ribbon:** (*select subregion of toposurface*) *Modify	Topography* tab> Subregion panel
	Edit Surface	• **Ribbon:** (*select toposurface*) *Modify	Topography* tab>Surface panel
	Graded Region	• **Ribbon:** *Massing & Site* tab>Modify Site panel
	Merge Surfaces	• **Ribbon:** *Massing & Site* tab>Modify Site panel
	Place Point	• **Ribbon:** *Modify	Edit Surface* tab> Tools panel
	Property Line	• **Ribbon:** *Massing & Site* tab>Modify Site panel
	Select Import Instance	• **Ribbon:** *Modify	Edit Surface* tab> Tools panel>Create from Import drop-down list
	Simplify Surface	• **Ribbon:** *Modify	Edit Surface* tab> Tools panel
	Specify Points File	• **Ribbon:** *Modify	Edit Surface* tab> Tools panel>Create from Import drop-down list
	Split Surface	• **Ribbon:** *Massing & Site* tab>Modify Site panel
	Subregion	• **Ribbon:** *Massing & Site* tab>Modify Site panel
	Toposurface	• **Ribbon:** *Massing & Site* tab>Model Site panel
Other Site-Related Tools		
	Label Contours	• **Ribbon:** *Massing & Site* tab>Modify Site panel
	Manage Links	• **Ribbon:** *Manage* tab>Manage Project panel
	Parking Component	• **Ribbon:** *Massing & Site* tab>Model Site panel
	Pick New Host	• **Ribbon:** *Modify	Component* tab> Host panel
	Site Component	• **Ribbon:** *Massing & Site* tab>Model Site panel
	Site Settings	• **Ribbon:** *Massing & Site* tab>Model Site panel title

⊕	**Spot Coordinate**	• **Ribbon:** *Annotate* tab>Dimension panel
⊕	**Spot Elevation**	• **Ribbon:** *Annotate* tab>Dimension panel

Index

www.ingramcontent.com/pod-product-compliance
Lightning Source LLC
Chambersburg PA
CBHW081542220326
41598CB00036B/6533